Brief Lives:
Geoffrey Chaucer

Brief Lives:
Geoffrey Chaucer

Gail Ashton

Brief Lives
Published by Hesperus Press Limited
19 Bulstrode Street, London W1U 2JN
www.hesperuspress.com

First published by Hesperus Press Limited, 2011

Designed and typeset by Fraser Muggeridge studio
Printed in Jordan by Jordan National Press

ISBN: 978-1-84391-918-6

Contents

Introduction

It's 9am, 14th December 1998. Jeremy Paxman is interviewing Jonathan Myerson, director of the BBC1 animated *Canterbury Tales* series (1998–2000), for BBC Radio 4's *Start the Week*. Myerson says of the *Tales,* 'Everyone feels in England a sort of sense of ownership about it but they haven't read it.' Just five days later the novelist Ian McEwan cites Geoffrey Chaucer as his 'person of the millennium' on Radio 4's *Today* programme. The UK millennium poll winner was, of course, William Shakespeare. Chaucer was not even shortlisted.

It seems Chaucer occupies a conflicted place in contemporary culture. If he is recognised at all it is as the author of a compressed and popularised *Canterbury Tales*, that notoriously argumentative pub-crawl perhaps best exemplified by 'The Miller's Tale' with its bums, farts and misdirected kisses. Chaucer also belongs to a nostalgic vision of a merrie England that never was, as well as being notable only by his absence in a fantasy of English Literature that begins – and sometimes even ends – with Shakespeare. The Chaucer of popular culture exists in tension with academic versions of the man and alongside constructions of a Chaucer gleaned from his life records and works: from fierce critic of the Church to conservative man of faith; Peter Ackroyd's 'new man'; and even, in Derek Pearsall's words, 'an honorary American' who transcends low birth through hard work and personal merit.

Chaucer was the first author writing in English to have his works collected into a single volume *and* one of the few named authors of his time. He acquired cultural centrality because other writers of the same period either slipped from view or, like John Gower, John Lydgate and William Langland, were accorded rather less institutional prestige. The so-called founding father of English poetry championed the use of English at a time when England's official language was French. His reputation as a poet and as a man was based, in part, upon pieces he never wrote. Whereas once he was modernised by writers like Pope, Wordsworth, and Elizabeth Barrett Browning, nowadays no poet of any literary standing undertakes such an enterprise.

This dizzying array of Chaucers is the subject of my biography. What we know of Chaucer is paradoxically both a little and a lot. We are more informed about him than about any of his contemporaries or about Shakespeare. Born into a family of merchants, he becomes an esquire and a controller of customs, and he carries out secret royal assignments. He is accused of rape. He enjoys the friendship of many powerful men, some of whom are later executed, and is rewarded by at least two kings despite the politically charged time in which he lives. While we continue to recognise Chaucer primarily as a poet, little information exists about his literary life. Where to find the man?

No life story is ever complete without its omissions, speculations and vested readings, and none more so than this. In some senses I begin with a death, paradoxically the point at which lives like Chaucer's take flight. In its aftermath are scores of afterlives, interpretations, even a cyberspace blog. It seems that with Chaucer at least, biography and critical discussion of his works are inseparable. Are we, as many have done, to look to his poetry to find something of his personality, his inclinations and beliefs? If so, how do we accommodate the Chaucer-persona or first-person narratives found there, how do we negotiate the complex and unique web of medieval manuscript culture and its material production? Conversely, what sort of *writer* Chaucer is has frequently been based on the construct of him as a *person*. 'Chaucer' is then a problematic set of assumptions, imaginings and projections that the gaps in his life history tempt us to fill in. The Chaucer I sketch in this book is but one version of a man who appears to us in many guises.

Origins
1340–60s

All stories have a beginning, or, in the case of biographies, a birth date. For a long time scholars believed that the medieval poet Geoffrey Chaucer was born in 1340. The legal archive of the famous medieval Scrope-Grosvenor court case of 1386, in which one Geoffrey Chaucer was witness number twenty-two, records that Chaucer states his age as 'forty years or more'. In that same document he also claims to have been 'armeez', that is a bearer of arms in royal service, for twenty-seven years. The existence of this document allows for a more recent estimation of 1343 as the likely year of Chaucer's birth, even though the phrase 'forty years or more' was merely a legal commonplace at that time while the bearing of arms might occur anywhere between the ages of sixteen and nineteen. Probably the best anyone can do is to say that Chaucer was born in the early 1340s.

We do know a little more about the world he was born into. Another legal document left over from the late medieval period sheds some light on Chaucer's place of birth and his immediate family connections. In a legal deed dated 19th June 1381, Geoffrey Chaucer relinquishes his rights to a tenement located in Thames Street, London. The house formerly belonged to Chaucer's father, described here as John Chaucer, vintner, and was undoubtedly left to Chaucer by his widowed mother after her death. The deed identifies John Chaucer as Geoffrey's parent for the first time and, so, allows us to trace his family tree.

Chaucer's family originally came from Ipswich, where they were most likely taverners. Chaucer's grandfather came to London as a vintner or wine merchant. The family name was actually Malin, not Chaucer. His paternal grandfather was variously known as Robert de Dynyngton, Robert Malyn, Robert Malyn le Chaucer and also Robert le Chaucer. Robert was apprenticed to a London merchant called John Chaucer. When this man died in 1302 Robert was named in his will. He inherited John Chaucer's business and, seemingly, assumed his name at the same time. This same Robert Chaucer was also in service to the King. He married Mary Heyron (Heron), a widow with one son, Thomas. Robert and Mary had a son of their own, John Chaucer (c. 1312–66), Geoffrey Chaucer's father. John wed Agnes de Coptin who was a ward and niece of the Keeper of the Royal Mint. They started a family – Geoffrey and possibly a girl called Katherine. According to Chaucer's *Life-Records*, she is mentioned just once, in a single document of 1619 when heraldic records identify a Katherine as the sister of the 'celebrated English poet, Geoffrey Chaucer'. The same Katherine is known to have been the wife of Simon Manning, someone for whom Chaucer acted as surety on 27th January 1386, which strengthens the possibility of a family connection. When Chaucer's grandfather died, his grandmother Mary married yet again, this time to another vintner – Robert's cousin Richard Chaucer. Chaucer's mother also remarried. Within a matter of weeks of John's death in 1366 she wed Bartholomew Chappel. Mary died in 1381, just before Chaucer sold the family house on Thames Street to a well-to-do Londoner, Henry Herbury.

Chaucer's family were not aristocrats but they were relatively prosperous and almost certainly aspirational, part of the newly emerging class of 'gentils', that prototype middle class composed of franklins, merchants, and royal and public servants that pervades *The Canterbury Tales*. In 1324, when Chaucer's father John was around twelve years old, he was abducted by a paternal aunt, Agnes de Westhale. At that time, Chaucer's grandmother

Mary had remarried, to their cousin Richard. Presumably John's aunt wanted John to marry her daughter Joan in order to secure inheritance for that branch of her family. The action was unsuccessful and John was awarded damages in 1330. Chaucer's father John reappears in the archives in 1328 when he and his step-brother Thomas Heron were involved in some sort of civic disturbance. It seems that the family was close, with Thomas allied both to John Chaucer and to the cousin, Richard, who married Chaucer's widowed grandmother, Thomas's mother. Certainly the Herons, the step-side of Chaucer's family, were linked in business with the Chaucers, for the Herons were wealthy pepperers trading in pepper, ginger, cinnamon, spices and other luxury commodities in a cosmopolitan area of London right next to where vintners like the Chaucers lived and worked.

Chaucer's family prospered through a combination of hard work, good fortune and preferment. By 1337 his father John was not only an important wine merchant but also in the service of the King, or so the *Life-Records* tell us. As deputy to the King's chief butler, John's job was to care for and maintain the royal wine cellars, a privileged position that set a precedent for Chaucer's own royal associations later on. By happy accident, John's service for the King took the entire family to Southampton in 1347. His job was to organise the collection of import duties on wine, something that kept them in Southampton for several years. Consequently, in 1349, the year that Black Death ravaged England and Europe, the Chaucers were out of London when disease hit the city. They all survived while the step-family branch of Herons was entirely wiped out. As a result, the Chaucers came into several properties on their return home later that same year. Soon John Chaucer was a freeman of the city of London, a man sufficiently well-reputed to be one of those who stood as surety in 1364 for a fellow vintner, the well-known merchant Richard Lyons. The guarantee was to ensure that Lyons occasioned no harm towards Alice Perrers, Edward

III's mistress, but perhaps more importantly it established a connection between the Chaucers and one of the most powerful men in London at that time. Significantly, Richard Lyons was the collector of the customs when, in 1374, Geoffrey Chaucer became controller there. Chaucer's father died in the early part of 1366. Although there is no trace of a will in any of the records, it seems likely that thanks to his father's prosperity as a vintner Chaucer inherited some wealth.

As far as we know, Chaucer was born in the same Thames Street house he sold in 1381. The purchaser, Henry Herbury, was a well-known and wealthy vintner who would have required a suitably imposing property, so it is reasonable to assume that Chaucer's home was fairly commodious. It had plenty of rooms, including underground cellars to store wine, and even a privy. Its address in Thames Street placed it in a central area of London known as the Vintry where wine merchants and traders of all nationalities, from Italian to French, Belgian and Flemish, might meet. Thames Street was also privileged by virtue of its position on the north side of the River Thames – hence the privy, which backed onto and over the river.

Beginnings
1350–60s

In the mini-biography attached to his 1598 edition of *Chaucer's Workes*, Thomas Speght claims that Chaucer and his friend and fellow poet John Gower were both educated at one of the famous Inns of Court. Speght says that Geoffrey Chaucer was fined two shillings for beating a friar in Fleet Street. Interesting though it is, the story is entirely apocryphal. It is possible, though, that at some point in his life he was loosely allied with one of the Inns via some informal instruction with a lawyer, or through his friendship with Gower and Ralph Strode, who was also a lawyer. This would certainly explain the extent of Chaucer's legal knowledge, which we witness everywhere in his works. Chaucer's later dealings at customs and an administrative career in which he was a trusted royal advocate – petitioning for a treaty with France in the Hundred Years War, for example – may also have given him a good working knowledge of the legal system. Similarly, as a mature man he was a Justice of the Peace, sat as an MP in at least one session of Parliament and frequently appears in judicial records in one way or another.

A single glance at Chaucer's literary output affirms that he was knowledgeable and widely read. Yet here we may well be misreading the nature of medieval textuality. The Latin tags, classical references, exemplary stories and so on that a poet like Chaucer uses would have been garnered from oral performances, moral homilies in church, printed stories like the compilations of friars, or encyclopedias by writers such as Vincent of Beauvais. Privately owned copies of manuscripts and anthologies were also circulated, loaned or exchanged as gifts via small audiences of courtiers, writers, or prosperous, book-collecting merchants. Most of these would have been annotated, glossed and commented upon by scribes and readers. As such, Chaucer's 'learning' is always mediated by others. Similarly, the medieval practice of 'auctoritas', which was required in all writing, detracts from any easy correlation between knowledge and formal education. All writers cited and referred to other authors or sources in order to enhance the authority of their work. These citations and illustrations were not necessarily taken from an original source. Rather, knowledge was often indirect, gleaned from other writers, translators and glossers. Chaucer no doubt knew Ovid, for instance, via the French translations of the classics like the *Ovid Moralisé*, while his English translation of Boethius's *The Consolation of Philosophy* – originally in Latin – probably came from *De Consolatione de Philosophique* by Jean de Meun and, in fact, stays close to large parts of that text.

The extent of Chaucer's formal education is, then, largely a matter of myth. We know that Chaucer was a page in the royal household while still a boy and it is here that his real education began. Not just anyone could become a page. All personal money was provided by the page's own family, while entry to the position was almost always the result of personal connections. Chaucer's father had begun to make inroads into the royal circle. Chaucer reaped the dividend and in a lucky break became a member of a royal household in spite of his inauspicious social background.

Pages were boys aged between ten and fourteen employed as servants and attendants in a household of note in return for free board and lodging, clothes and other necessaries. They needed to become fully literate and, so, were probably taught grammar, rhetoric and enough formal legal discourse (often in Latin or French) to manage official documents. A page had to have a sound working knowledge of several languages, including the 'high' French of the royal house. Given Chaucer's later career – his diplomatic missions abroad, connection via marriage with the Hainault region of Normandy, his posts at customs, which demanded a commercial patois of English, French, Italian, Dutch and Flemish, plus his poetry – we can assume that he excelled in this area. Pages also inhabited royal and aristocratic society and so they were taught court manners, the art of courtesy, of diplomacy, conversation, music, singing, dancing, hawking and hunting. Their contact with court entertainment, its readings, recitations, minstrelsy and performances, was extensive. In addition, most – like Chaucer – were 'armeez', taught to fight and expected to go into the field of battle.

Two leaves accidentally attached to the binding of another book allow us a glimpse of this young Chaucer. They survive as part of the household accounts of Elizabeth, Countess of Ulster and wife of Prince Lionel, Edward III's second surviving son. The record covers the period of July 1356 to January 1359, and mentions Chaucer by name. The accounts show that on a day in 1357 'Galfrido Chaucer' received a pair of shoes and a pair of red and black hose. On exactly the same day a further payment of a 'paltok', a cloak of the type medieval pages wore, was made to the same person. This is the first clear sign that Chaucer was a page in the Countess's service. Later records show other payments and gifts, mainly for clothes of the sort required for various royal occasions or aristocratic feasts and activities.

We do not know for how long Chaucer was a page. As was usual for the time, the Countess of Ulster kept a separate house from that of her husband. She managed her own financial affairs and appointed attendants of her choice. The records for her household end in the autumn of 1359 when Prince Lionel came of age and merged his household with that of his wife. It is fair to assume that Chaucer became a page just before that first appearance in Elizabeth's accounts and was probably one not much beyond the point at which records cease. Equally, it is likely that when the households of Elizabeth and Lionel combined, Chaucer became Lionel's page or attendant, and that as he matured he moved up the ranks to become what records variously describe as 'valettus' (yeoman of the chamber) or 'esquire'. A number of documents testify to these claims.

If we return for a moment to the famous Scrope-Grosvenor dispute of 1359, we may recall that Chaucer describes himself as 'armeez' or 'armed'. The large sum of money (£16) paid for his ransom on 1st March 1360, after he was captured in France while on the King's service as part of the ongoing hostilities of the Hundred Years War, confirms this fact. Chaucer was part of a small company led by Prince Lionel, Earl of Ulster in France to campaign – unsuccessfully as it happens – for Edward III's alleged right to the French Crown. This military endeavour took place in 1359–60 and ended with the Treaty of Brétigny in the autumn of that latter year, a formal event attended by Chaucer according to surviving accounts of it. The records for that trip also mention by name the following: Prince Lionel, his brother Edward of Woodstock, known as the Black Prince, and one 'Galfrido Chaucer' who was paid nine shillings for carrying letters to England. In short, we know that Chaucer had improved his social standing, was now in Lionel's service and an active and valued advocate – hence the ransom – of royal business.

After October 1360 and right up until 1365 Chaucer's life story becomes largely a matter of conjecture. There are large gaps in the archives, silences that sit uneasily beside a handful of recorded events and adversely affect the clarity of some remaining documents. At some point, for example, Chaucer left the household of the Ulsters. Prince Lionel was in Ireland during the summer of 1361, where he stayed on and off until late 1366 in an attempt to bring that country under complete English rule. We know, too, that Elizabeth accompanied him and that she died shortly after in 1363. What we don't know is what Chaucer was doing at this time or where he was exactly during these five or six years.

Most scholars suspect that he was in the service of another royal household, possibly in England or, more likely, in Aquitaine, France. The royal archives at Navarre in Spain only relatively recently yielded a passage for safe conduct issued for the period 22nd February to 24th May 1366, and recorded in the *Life-Records* as given to one *'Geffroy de Chauserre escuier englois en sa compagnie trios compaignons'* (Geoffrey Chaucer, English esquire, accompanied by three others). The nature of Chaucer's business is not recorded. Pilgrims en route to the famous shrine of St James of Compostella had to pass through Navarre. Some believe that Chaucer was one of them. Yet the period specified falls during Lent, not part of the usual pilgrimage season. It is more likely that Chaucer was on unofficial royal business as part of a secret mission and, so, no reason is stated on the safe conduct pass.

The timing does coincide though with a threat to Pedro of Castile from France. English forces had already sided with Pedro against the French in order to secure his crown and retain him as a crucial ally in the Hundred Years War. Was Chaucer sent to rally English soldiers based in France as part of the ongoing war between the two nations, and, perhaps, to instruct them to come to the aid of Castile? Alternatively, Chaucer's presence in Spain may have been part of a plan to keep Charles of Navarre on side in the continuing military action there. Whatever the truth, it seems that Chaucer's 'lost' years were spent in France in the service of Lionel's brother, the Black Prince, Edward III's heir.

What Kind of Man Are You?

'what man artow?' quod he;
'Thou lookest as thou woldest fynde an hare,
For evere upon the ground I se thee stare.'
The Canterbury Tales, VII, 695–7

These days most of us judge a book by its cover. Browsing the three-for-two tables of major bookshops we may find ourselves drawn towards an attractive dust jacket with its tantalising blurb and sound-bite reviews. We make our choice, perhaps glancing through title pages with their assertion of copyright, definitive list of other publications, a short author biography, even a photograph of the writer, for in spite of a postmodern emphasis upon the death of the cult of the author, we like to know something of the men and women who write what we read. How might a twenty-first-century publishing world package Geoffrey Chaucer? Several major works are unfinished: *The Canterbury Tales*, *The House of Fame* and *The Legend of Good Women*. Geoffrey Chaucer will *not* have asserted his rights in accordance with any known notion of copyright. And what of the author? Geoffrey Chaucer is a civil servant, diplomat and royal spy who lives and works in London and Kent. He is married with two or maybe three children. He has been dead for over six hundred years.

Surprisingly, we have a picture to accompany this imaginary Chaucer book. Or rather we have several extant possibilities from an age when portraiture was unusual. When it occurred at all in medieval culture – and this was rare, especially in England – the depictions were often vague or idealised. Medieval portraits were composed with allegory in mind, not verisimilitude. Nonetheless, several pictures stake a claim as representations of Chaucer and do so in ways that at least seem to be lifelike. Possibly the most famous of these is the one accompanying most modern editions of his works, that is the portly, genial-looking chap seated on a horse and situated either near the fictional Tabard Inn belonging to Harry Bailly, the Host of *The Canterbury Tales*, or as part of an imaginary pilgrimage en route to the shrine of Thomas à Beckett in Canterbury Cathedral. This image is taken from the detailed thumb-print of what is allegedly a portrait of Geoffrey Chaucer. It is the same as the one found in the margins of the most well-known and frequently used 'base' copy of *The Canterbury Tales*, which is the Ellesmere manuscript of the Huntington Library in San Marino, California (known as MSEL 26. C.9). Here, just as with all the other tale-telling pilgrims of *The Canterbury Tales* collection, the illustration marks the beginning of Chaucer's own story – in this case 'The Tale of Melibee' and not 'The Tale of Sir Thopas', which a character called Chaucer also recounts as part of the fictional story-telling contest that partially frames *The Canterbury Tales*.

A similar drawing of Chaucer occurs in another early fifteenth-century manuscript – MS Harley 486, currently held in the British Library, London. It is attached to Thomas Hoccleve's *Regement of Princes*, which was written somewhere between 1411 and 1412, a decade or so after Chaucer's death. The actual Harley manuscript was begun in the early 1400s. It was commissioned by Henry, Prince of Wales, later Henry V, and may even have been made as a presentation copy for him. What is startling about the Harley portrait is that Hoccleve clearly intends it as an iconic image of remembrance for the 'master' poet who came before him and that it is claimed as an actual likeness. Hoccleve concludes his *Regement of Princes* with a eulogy of Geoffrey Chaucer.

At some point he recalls that his audience may not have known the man of whom he writes, and so he offers this true-to-life picture as a kind of memorial.

Hoccleve's insistence that this is a genuine likeness is probably truthful given that he presents it when the poet was still in living memory for some. The similarity of the Harley and the Ellesmere pictures might also suggest that the depiction of Chaucer was an accurate one. Both the Harley and the Ellesmere portraits reproduce similar facial features and other details. They show a serious-looking Chaucer with a 'penner' or pen-case around his neck to denote his profession as a writer. Both strike the same pose with his hands held before him, one raised as if pointing and the other lower, seemingly grasping something. In the Ellesmere manuscript this is the hand that holds the reins of his horse, while in Harley Chaucer has a rosary entwined in his fingers. No-one knows which came first. Was the Ellesmere drawing taken directly from the Harley image or were both based on another picture familiar to Hoccleve and others?

Chaucer's likeness crops up elsewhere in the early 1400s in, for instance, an illustrated frontispiece to a copy of his *Troilus and Criseyde*, where, apart from the fact that he is standing at a lectern reciting verse, he clearly resembles those other early depictions. Whatever the truth, Hoccleve's intent to commemorate had results. Its legacy was that picture of Chaucer that is familiar even to contemporary audiences and which has endured despite the fact that of the forty copies of the *Regement* that survive, scarcely any replicate Hoccleve's 'original'. Nevertheless, the inclusion of Chaucer's image – regardless of its veracity – soon became traditional.

The desire to put a name to a face is, of course, entirely natural. Perhaps this is why so many scholars have been eager to search the archives and why so many of us scan Chaucer's features – if, indeed, they are his – for any trace of the human Geoffrey. Yet as ever with Chaucer, we can take nothing at face value. Geoffrey's picture decorates his tomb in Westminster

Abbey alongside a now illegible inscription on one of the arches that supports the marble canopy erected by Nicholas Brigham in 1556. Another finds its way into Thomas Speght's editions of Chaucer's collected *Workes* (1598, 1602, 1687). Speght includes a picture of the author on the 'Progenie' or lineage page in these folios. The Progenie illustration was specially engraved for the *Workes* by John Speed, who positions it above the tomb of Thomas Chaucer, Geoffrey's son, and between two family trees – that of the Chaucers and, interestingly given my later suppositions about Thomas's parentage, that of John of Gaunt. A similar depiction frequently serves as a frontispiece for numerous collections of Chaucer's works by other editors.

That small round man with the friendly face persists today. Nowadays, he does not have a rosary, sign of a piety that looks to recuperate him from accusations of Lollard tendencies and reclaim him for Catholicism despite the condemnation of the medieval Church in his writing. Instead he rides his horse towards Canterbury, a pilgrim in his own story, or lurks near a hostelry as if about to invite us on an inebriated jolly through 'merrie Englande'. Geoffrey Chaucer has other faces too. He gazes back at us from a number of library portraits hanging in the stately homes of places such as Stanshawes Court in Gloucestershire, Scotland's Bothwell Castle, Longleat House in Wiltshire and Knole in Kent, or else graces the galleries of libraries like Oxford's Bodleian or the university collections of Harvard, California and Columbia. This Geoffrey Chaucer has a more patrician countenance as befits the 'father' of English poetry.

Alternatively, most notably in Victorian and Edwardian books for children, Chaucer is the 'popet' – or 'little doll' – of the Host's description in *The Canterbury Tales*. All of this is in contrast to the elegant, bookish fellow of a few decades earlier conjured in William Morris's famously extravagant 'Kelmscott' edition of Chaucer's works. There Chaucer is illustrated by Morris's friend and fellow Pre-Raphaelite Edward Burne-Jones.

This Chaucer is integrated into a Pre-Raphaelite artistic vision: slimmer than in the Harley-Ellesemere tradition and with more aquiline features.

The Kelmscott volume opens with this 'new' Chaucer seemingly writing in a book. He is alone and looks refined and thoughtful. This is the Chaucer read through the dream-visions, his *Parliament of Fowls*, *The Book of the Duchess*, *The House of Fame* and the Prologue to *The Legend of Good Women*, poems in which the studious first-person narrator reads throughout the night and stands on the fringes of life with no personal experience of love or the hurly-burly of the outside world worth mentioning. The dream-vision poems imagine, too, a writer devoted to flowers and knee-deep in daisies, the nature poet so admired by the Romantics and constructed through an apocryphal Chaucer canon that was not excised until long after Morris and Burne-Jones dedicated the Kelmscott book to Geoffrey Chaucer. Edward Burne-Jones is said to have been inspired in his art by Chaucer's 'Cuckoo and Nightingale' – which Chaucer did not actually write. Burne-Jones also assumed that Chaucer translated the French *Romance of the Rose* into English despite doubts in other quarters of nineteenth-century culture, and illustrates his 'Chaucer' accordingly. Thus paintings of the same unworldly character in dreamy contemplation of the rose link the end of *The Rose* and the start of *The Parliament of Fowls* via a symmetrical two-page spread.

The gentleman-aesthete Chaucer is largely confined to the Victorian Kelmscott volume. The early 1930s return us to Hoccleve's iconic portrait of the genial humanist, but this time with an additional twist. G.K. Chesterton's construction of Chaucer as the founding father of an English nation was highly influential. Chesterton's 'portrait', described in his 1932 volume *Chaucer*, is an imaginary one sketched in the shape of a giant and imprinted on the landscape of England, deep in its very fabric and condition. The vision is, he says, best appreciated from an aerial perspective not unlike that of the eagle in *The*

House of Fame, which carries 'Chaucer' on its back and encourages him to look upon the world below. In our mind's eye, too, we might glance down and see 'our native hills for his bones and our native forests for his beard; and see... a single figure outlined against the sea, and a great face staring at the sky'.

Man on the Move
1366–78

Where does a royal servant like Chaucer fit in a late medieval world? Somewhere between 1366 and 1368 he moved up a rank to become 'esquire', one of those emergent 'gentils', those prosperous and increasingly influential people who, though not noble by birth, were sufficiently upwardly mobile to ensure their place immediately below the aristocracy and far above the 'commons' or ordinary men and women. In royal records dated 20th June 1367 Chaucer is still named as 'valettus' in the service of Edward III. The King granted him a life annuity of twenty marks – around £14 in old money – to be paid in twice-yearly instalments. This was a usual reward for royal servants and also one that was actually paid, at least until Chaucer decided to sell it on in 1388. It confirms what we already know, that Chaucer must have left the service of Prince Lionel and the Countess Elizabeth some time earlier, and that he had been promoted to 'valettus' for some time; the annuity was offered *'pro bono servicio'* (for good service). It may even have marked the occasion of Chaucer becoming an esquire, the term most often cited in the records next to his name.

Like pages, esquires received payment and clothes for special occasions. Royal livery was one of several signs of prestigious attachment to a royal household. Chaucer's name appears in a number of documents recording such gifts. In November 1368, 'Geoffrey Chaucer' was one of forty esquires given Christmas robes. Similarly, he received clothing in the Whitsun of 1369 and, again, in autumn of that same year – along with his wife Philippa – for the funeral of Edward III's Queen Philippa. Documents even suggest that at some point Chaucer was part of that elevated rank of esquires attached not merely to the King's household but to the King's chamber. These servants were part of the King's inner sanctum, his *secreta familia* who travelled everywhere with him and were in constant attendance. Records for 1371–3 note that Chaucer is one of these *'scutiferis camere regis'*; accordingly, he received a number of winter and summer robes during these years.

This particularly privileged occupation presumably ended around 1374 when Chaucer was appointed as controller of the customs. Thus he was no longer able to travel with the royal household or fulfil the requirement of living at court. Nor is he necessarily listed in subsequent records alongside other esquires. Yet Chaucer is sometimes called 'esquier' (esquire) elsewhere, suggesting he remained in royal service in a variety of ways. Wardrobe and sumptuary accounts for 1376–7 record that he is owed money for expenditure on robes. Chaucer is also mentioned as one of many esquires granted livery for mourning Joan of Kent, Edward's mother, in 1385. The life annuity Edward III granted Chaucer in 1367 came with a demand to serve when required and to be present on special or particular occasions. It seems, then, that Chaucer still retained his post of esquire of the King's household but did not continue in his role as a member of the King's chamber.

Geoffrey Chaucer was a trusted royal servant and diplomat right up until his death. In 1374 Edward III granted him a daily pitcher of wine, a gift equivalent to a gallon or a staggering four and a half litres every single day. A few years later in 1378 Chaucer swapped this for an annuity of twenty marks, to be paid by the exchequer in addition to his earlier annuity from the King for the same sum. Chaucer also travelled abroad on numerous occasions as an ambassador for the royal household. The *Life-Records* tell how the royal privy seal issued a warrant on 17th July 1368 for *'nostre ame valet Geffrey Chaucer'*. This permitted foreign travel, for which Chaucer was also given two horses and enough money – twenty shillings plus £10 in the medieval equivalent of travellers' cheques to cash in at Calais – to get him to anywhere in Europe. Both his destination and the nature of his business are unknown.

Around September 1369 he was given a 'prest', a £10 advance to defray the cost of a journey made as an esquire in the King's household. On 20th June of the following year Chaucer received letters of protection enabling him to travel abroad in, as the records phrase it, the service of the King. Once again, the precise nature of Chaucer's remit goes unrecorded. Most historians assume it involves England's continued war with France. John of Gaunt, with whom Chaucer was closely associated, led an unsuccessful expedition to France after renewed hostilities in 1369.

In December 1372 Chaucer was part of a trading mission sent to Genoa in Italy. The trip received a large advance for expenses. Chaucer's statement for expenditure for the period 1st December 1372 to 23rd May 1373 still exists. This record indicates that he spent around three months in Italy, excluding travel, and also clearly notes him as *'armigero regis'* for the first time; that is esquire of the royal household. The purpose of the trip was to negotiate with the Genoese for a special English seaport exclusively for Genoese merchants, although some think it might also have involved securing mercenaries to assist Edward's soldiers in France. Chaucer's presence was undoubtedly crucial, not least because of his proficiency in Italian and established contacts with Italian merchants, both gained through his family's commercial background. Trade accounts of subsequent years suggest that the mission was a success.

In the years of 1376 through to 1378, Chaucer's international diplomatic role was at its height, even though he now had a new post as controller of the wool customs at the city port. Ambassadors customarily received special treatment so these foreign trips greatly enhanced Chaucer's social standing. He visited France on a number of occasions, first of all to treat for peace and later on a related venture to petition a French princess for marriage to the teenage Richard II. Richard Stury, one of the King's chamber knights and Chaucer's friend, and Guichard d'Angle, Richard's tutor until 1372, both accompanied him on that second occasion. Chaucer was somewhere in France (only his expenses sheet survives) during 1376 and on four occasions in 1377 as efforts to end the Hundred Years War intensified. On 17th February 1377, as with all of his other trips, he was given a large advance for travel to Flanders. The receipts he submitted on his return indicate that Chaucer had also been in Paris and Montreuil.

England's domestic situation changed dramatically during these years. In 1376 Edward's heir, the Black Prince, died, followed a year later by Edward himself. The new King was the Black Prince's eleven-year-old son Richard, who ascended the throne in 1378. Yet Chaucer continued to prove an asset to the Crown. In that same year, Chaucer was sent to Lombardy, Italy accompanied by a Sir Edward Berkeley. Chaucer was out of England, and absent from his job in charge of the wool customs, from 28th May to 14th September 1378. The entourage visited Bernabò Visconti, the powerful ruler of Milan, and Sir John Hawkwood, the famous English mercenary and Visconti's son-in-law. Chaucer was to commend the young King Richard II to Visconti, perhaps to persuade him to offer financial support to the continued struggle with France and also to propose Richard's marriage yet again, this time to Visconti's daughter Caterina. Two Milanese ambassadors returned with Chaucer to England that same year carrying formal marriage papers and a significant dowry as testament to the success of that part of the operation, at least. When Richard II eventually married Anne of Bohemia, the English court began to be famed for its cosmopolitan sophistication and championing of the arts. These were to be good omens for Geoffrey Chaucer.

Private Lives
1357–87

Christmas, 1357. Prince Lionel and his wife Elizabeth, Countess of Ulster, are celebrating at their home in Hatfield, Yorkshire. The records tell of a gift of clothes to their page Geoffrey Chaucer who was, we assume, present at this Yuletide feast. Other names of note appear on the guest list for these festivities. Lionel's seventeen-year-old brother the Earl of Richmond, better known as John of Gaunt, is there. Their mother Queen Philippa of Hainault is known to have presided over this royal Christmas. Most probably she brought with her ladies-in-waiting, one of whom was the girl who became Chaucer's wife. Records note the mysterious 'Philippa Pan', believed to be one of the de Roet girls who hailed from the same region of France as the Queen. The daughter of Henry, Duke of Lancaster, also seems to have attended the party. Blanche would become John of Gaunt's first wife and, later, the dedicatee of Chaucer's commemorative poem *The Book of the Duchess*. Also listed is the name of Katherine de Roet. She wed Hugh of Swynford but was Gaunt's mistress throughout his subsequent marriage to Constance of Castile in 1372, if not before. Katherine had one son with Hugh and a number of children with Gaunt. John of Gaunt and Katherine were finally married in 1396 after Constance died. This same Katherine was Philippa's sister and, hence, Chaucer's sister-in-law.

This Christmas event may well have been the first meeting of a group of people who were to be inextricably connected for several decades to come. John of Gaunt (d. 1399) was Edward III's third son. He rapidly became one of the most powerful figures of the late medieval age, both in his own right and as advisor to his young nephew Richard II, who succeeded Edward. As well as the party at Hatfield in 1357, we know that Gaunt and Chaucer crossed paths on military expeditions to France in 1359 and again in 1369 and also, most probably, at the battle of Najera, Spain, in 1367. Gaunt's long-standing relationship with Katherine Swynford further embedded an association with Chaucer and has undoubtedly encouraged speculation over the state of Chaucer's emotional life. Did Gaunt also bed Katherine's sister and so sire Chaucer's own children? Was this the reason why Philippa later moved to Lincoln to be with Katherine and their extended family of half-siblings and stepson? Gaunt certainly seems to have enjoyed keeping his paramours and wives in close proximity. Katherine was foster mother to his children by Blanche. Philippa was later in service to his second wife Constance and also part of Katherine's household in Lincoln for a number of years: as Katherine's sister or as a former lover and mother to his children? Was Chaucer's marriage a convenience that left him free to pursue his own life and even set up a ménage à trois with Cecily Champain (Champaigne), of whom I have more to say later?

During those years in which Chaucer's name disappears from all records we know only that some time before 1366 he married Philippa de Roet, lady-in-waiting to the Queen. On 12th September 1366 Philippa is documented as receiving a life annuity for her service to Edward III's consort and her fellow Hainault. Both Philippa and Chaucer are mentioned on a number of separate occasions verifying that they were part of the same social group. It is not until the autumn of 1368 that their names appear together as husband and wife. Like many others, someone described as 'Geffrey Chaucer' was given robes to wear at Queen Philippa's state funeral. This time the name of the Queen's lady-in-waiting is not Philippa de Roet but 'Philippa Chaucer'. If, as seems likely, Philippa is the 'Philippa Pan' of the 1357 household accounts of the Countess of Ulster, then Geoffrey Chaucer made a highly advantageous marriage. The reference to Pan matches the name of Paon (Payne) de Roet, an eminent aristocrat from the same Hainault region of France as Edward's Queen Philippa. Chaucer's wife and Katherine Sywnford were Paon's daughters. So, too, Philippa de Roet was a member of the Queen's inner household and later John of Gaunt's via her service to his second wife Constance of Castile. She was also his mistress's sister. Chaucer himself was, at best, an esquire, not a knight like his new father-in-law, and certainly not in possession of any land.

History has little to say about Philippa, especially in regard to her status as Chaucer's wife. We know that she received an annual pension of twenty marks for service to the queen and that in 1372 she was granted an additional £10, this time from John of Gaunt for service to his wife Constance. Philippa was among those given gifts when Gaunt left England in 1373 for manoeuvres in France. On his return a year later, Philippa joined Gaunt and Constance in semi-exile at Tutbury Castle, Staffordshire. We know too that both of her annuities were regularly paid and on time, not directly to her but to her assigned payee Geoffrey Chaucer. As a public administrator Chaucer would have had intimate knowledge of the dilatory workings of the royal pensions system and was probably acquainted with its officials. The arrangement was undoubtedly pragmatic but, of course, it reveals nothing of the relationship between him and his wife. The couple lived separately for large parts of the year as did many royal servants. They had no place of their own until Chaucer was offered the lease on the Aldgate house mentioned earlier. This was in 1374, some ten years after their marriage. Yet during the 1380s Philippa spent most of her time with Gaunt's wife Constance, as evidenced by records of payment of New Year's gifts from Constance to Philippa in 1380, 1381 and 1382. After that there are no more records of any kind for Gaunt's household. Gaunt, Constance and, interestingly, Chaucer's young son Thomas – who was a page for Gaunt at this time – decamped with their entourage to Spain during the years 1386–9. Philippa did not, as might be expected, accompany them.

Neither did she move to cohabit with her husband. Released from service – or so it would appear – she moved to Lincolnshire to be with her sister Katherine. Philippa seems to have been living there, when not required to be with Constance, from 1379 onwards. A warrant for payment of the half-yearly instalment of one of Philippa's annuities was made to Gaunt's receiver in Lincoln in the second half of 1379, just as a year earlier it had fallen to the Sheriff of Lincoln. In 1386 Philippa was admitted into the fraternity of Lincoln Cathedral. The occasion, which fell in February of that year, was a large family gathering, one that offers further evidence of the complex affiliations of Chaucer's private life. John of Gaunt's eldest son Henry, Earl of Derby, and later Henry IV, became a member of the cathedral at the same time as Philippa, following in the footsteps of Gaunt himself and *his* father before him. John of Gaunt was present at the event alongside Katherine Swynford, Philippa's sister. They were witnessing the admittance of their eldest, John of Beaufort, Henry's illegitimate half-brother, and also that of Katherine's son with Hugh Swynford, Thomas. Surprisingly, there is no mention of Chaucer at all.

His absence is rather puzzling. This was a significant event for all of those concerned and clearly something the 'family' wished to mark. Chaucer was in England at the time yet did not appear at his wife's side. In the autumn Chaucer collected both his and Philippa's annuities in person, while just a month before the Lincoln Cathedral gathering he stood surety for his brother-in-law Simon Manning. Conversely, it seems that Philippa had for some years prior to this occasion failed to take opportunities to be with her husband. Did something more than work commitments prompt this apparent rift? Chaucer was, after all, in semi-hiding in Kent at this time looking to avoid the Lords Appellant, and with good reason as we shall shortly see. Or were Chaucer and Philippa separated, the marriage – if it ever truly was one – having run its course? A few years earlier Chaucer had been charged with rape, a case that has always aroused much scholarly controversy and speculation and something that is the subject of a later chapter. Was this the reason for his apparent estrangement from his wife, or was John of Gaunt seeking to recognise his mistresses the de Roet sisters, and both his and their numerous offspring? Perhaps the matter is simpler still, that ill-health prompted Philippa's retirement from royal service and a desire to lead a more reclusive life with just her sister for company. A year later, somewhere between June and November of 1387, all payments to Philippa cease and she disappears from the records, presumably dead.

Some say that Geoffrey and Philippa had two daughters and one, maybe two, sons. An Agnes Chaucer was an attendant at the coronation of Henry V and there is a Lewis in the records of whom I have more to say later. We know for definite only of an Elizabeth and a son, Thomas, whose name frequently appears in the archives; for, like his father before him, Thomas was a highly effective courtier and politician. Thomas was born in 1367 and was placed in the service of John of Gaunt at an early age, a position that was made a life-long appointment in 1389. His success continued when Gaunt's son, Henry Bolingbroke, made him Constable of Wallingford just three days after his coronation as Henry IV. In 1400 Thomas became a sheriff in Oxfordshire and a knight of the shire a year later. Thomas followed in his father's footsteps by becoming an MP. He represented the county of Oxfordshire on many occasions and was also elected Speaker on no fewer than five occasions (1407, 1410, 1411, 1414 and 1421). Though he later refused a full knighthood, there is no doubting Thomas Chaucer's renown. Like his father, Thomas survived three kingships. Though his dedicated support to the house of Gaunt was well rewarded by Bolingbroke, Thomas was soon highly critical of Henry and switched allegiance to the Prince of Wales. He acted as a diplomat for Henry V and was later given a seat in the largely aristocratic council of Henry VI.

Thomas Chaucer was his father's son, and more. Marriage to Maud Burghersh, the daughter and sole heir of Sir John Burghersh of Ewelme, brought him a number of estates in Surrey and great prestige. The marriage was arranged by John of Gaunt, perhaps for no other reason than partiality of kinship – Thomas's aunt was Katherine Swynford, Gaunt's lover and, later, third wife – or reward for loyal service. Or did something else bind Thomas and the Lancasters? Depicted on Thomas Chaucer's tomb is the coat of arms of the de Roets, the family of his mother. We might expect to see his father's coat of arms too, if he had one – which as a mere esquire Chaucer would not. Yet the *Life-Records* reveal some surprising evidence to suggest that Thomas did, in fact, inherit arms from his father. This is in the form of a seal that Thomas used in 1409. The inscription on it is difficult to decipher; it seems to read 'Ghofrai [?] Chavcier'. On the back is a distinctive shield. In the fifteenth and sixteenth centuries this emblem was commonly assumed to belong to Geoffrey Chaucer. So, if Thomas inherited his father's coat of arms, why are they not displayed in the usual manner of late medieval tombstones?

Some think that Chaucer's arms were simply not sufficiently eminent and this is why the arms of the de Roets quarter those of his wife's family, the Burghershs. Might this rather odd heraldic display have a more salacious reason? Some suppose that Thomas and Elizabeth were not actually Chaucer's children at all but John of Gaunt's bastards. This would explain why Chaucer's coat of arms is missing and account for the favouritism Thomas received in the way of marriage and position long after Gaunt's death. John of Gaunt also paid for Thomas's sister Elizabeth to join the London Order of Black Nuns in 1381. It is true that Gaunt was known for his generosity to loyal retainers. But, given the question marks over Chaucer's private life with Philippa, the idea that Geoffrey Chaucer merely conferred legitimacy on yet more of Gaunt's children remains exceptionally interesting, if probably ultimately unlikely.

Danger in London
1374–86

The latter years of the 1370s were a challenging time for an ambitious man like Geoffrey Chaucer. As Edward III's life drew to a close his increasing senility created a power vacuum and much in-fighting. His mistress Alice Perrers exerted a not inconsiderable influence, while a number of wealthy London merchants strengthened their fiscal ties to the royal court. In 1374 Chaucer was appointed controller of the wool custom and wool subsidy at the port of London. Although this was a paid position it was not especially prestigious or one usually associated with aspiring courtiers. In his biography of Chaucer, Derek Pearsall supposes that Chaucer accepted the post in order to distance himself from instability at court. He adds that an 'intelligent man' like Chaucer would be aware of the potential danger of continued association with merchants like his father's friend Richard Lyons, and so begin to drift away from the city.

Yet several factors undermine Pearsall's assumption. Richard Lyons was, in fact, Chaucer's superior at the customs; indeed, it is highly likely that Chaucer gained his own position through preferment, through his father's association with Lyons. It is true that Lyons was one of those accused of profiteering in the 1376 parliament but, by then, he was no longer Chaucer's boss, having been jailed within two years of Chaucer's appointment, most probably for malpractice. On 10th May 1374 Chaucer was granted a life-long, rent-free lease on an imposing dwelling over the city gate at Aldgate. This was a significant favour. When Chaucer eventually left the house in 1386, for instance, the lease passed to another well-reputed royal esquire Richard Forester, while Chaucer's friend Ralph Strode occupied a similar house. Though the residence belonged to the city rather than to the King, Chaucer's acceptance of it coincides with Edward III's gift of the daily pitcher of wine (later transferred to an annuity) and the reaffirmation of his links to the Lancastrian household of Edward's son, John of Gaunt. On his return from that failed expedition to France mentioned earlier, Gaunt sought to re-establish his former power base in England. Accordingly, in April of 1374 he presented grants to men close to Chaucer, like Richard Stury, Sir Lewis Clifford and Philip de la Vache. The very day after Chaucer was sworn in as controller of customs, he accepted Gaunt's offer of an annuity of £10. And, of course, throughout his time as controller, and, indeed, for the rest of his life, Chaucer remained an esquire continuing with his diplomatic and ambassadorial trips abroad, sometimes on secret business, for both Edward III and his successor Richard II. It seems, then, highly unlikely that Chaucer viewed his new position as an opportunity to withdraw from the complex web of association and cronyism that characterised late medieval court life.

From at least 1376 onwards Chaucer's various annuities were paid via his customs post. In addition, the job proved a valuable stepping-stone to other, more prestigious offices later in his career. It is entirely possible too that the wool subsidy position incorporated several associated aspects of customs officialdom. On 20th April 1382 Chaucer was officially appointed controller of petty customs, a task he had probably already undertaken. He was now responsible for charging the correct export duty on wool, leather and other goods, as well as collecting the petty customs 'tax'. He had to be on duty at all times and mediate any disputes. He was required to keep all administration in proper order, complete with correct documentation and records written in his own hand *saunz fauxme or fraude'* – without falsehood or fraud. None survives. Both controllerships were subject to the superior position of controller of customs. This was the person who actually kept the customs payments, usually an influential merchant – Richard Lyons, for example – or one to whom the Crown was obligated in some way. Chaucer's role clearly demanded a measure of accommodation or circumspection since the controllership was susceptible to financial irregularity and always held by someone of higher rank.

Chaucer's position at petty customs allowed him to appoint a deputy at any time, something he took advantage of in 1383, for instance, while away on personal, unknown business, then for an entire month in 1384 when on King's business abroad, and again on 13th December 1386 when he left his deputy Henry Gisors in charge. Even before this, every time Chaucer's diplomatic envoys took him overseas he relinquished control to his deputies. There is, for example, a handwritten note in French, dated 1378, which records the name of Richard Barrett as temporary wool customs controller; the writing may even be Chaucer's own. In fact, it seems that Chaucer's deputies were in almost permanent charge as early as February 1385, Chaucer having given up all day-to-day administration save for management of the accounts. By 1386, when Chaucer completely resigned both the wool and petty customs controllerships, he had been in office for twelve years; only one controller had ever been in post for longer.

The years 1380–6 were especially favourable to Geoffrey Chaucer. At this time he was around forty years of age, a man who held remunerated and highly visible office as a customs official. He occupied a commodious house in London on which he paid no rent. His friends were influential, respected men. He was in receipt of royal annuities in recognition of his work as an esquire and probably still received a small pension from John of Gaunt who was the uncle of, and by that time a key advisor to, the young King Richard. But change was in the air and the political turbulence of the 1380s undoubtedly played a part in Chaucer's decision to resign.

The so-called Peasants' Revolt of 1381 incurred full-scale rioting and violence of all kinds, including an arson attack on John of Gaunt's palace at the Savoy. The protest was sparked by a punitive poll tax designed, in part, to raise revenue for the Hundred Years War. The fourteen-year-old King favoured peace with France, because of the war's exorbitant cost and because he wanted to centralise the monarchy. His barons disagreed; the tax was actually the brainchild of Richard's uncles John of Gaunt and Thomas Woodstock. The rebels entered the city of London after an insider unlocked some of its gates. Aldgate was one of these gates, and Chaucer's house was above it. The King promised to grant all the demands of the protestors and brought signed pardons before leading them onto Clerkenwell fields from where they dispersed. Within hours they were hunted down and executed in what Terry Jones calls in his book *Who Murdered Chaucer?* one of 'the bloodiest reprisals in English history'. Most assume that Chaucer was absent from the city at the time of the insurgence, though there is no evidence to prove the case either way, nor any way of knowing if he witnessed events first hand or simply heard about the attempted rebellion. It may even be coincidence that just a few days later the house in St Martin, Vintry that Chaucer inherited from his parents was passed by deed to Henry Herbury. By the autumn of 1386, Chaucer had renounced the lease on the Aldgate residence altogether and moved to Kent into semi-hiding.

Rape and Writs
1380–88

In 1380 Chaucer was accused of rape. In a document dated 1st May a woman described only as 'Cecilia Champaigne' (Cecily Champain) offers one Geoffrey Chaucer an unconditional release from 'all actions concerning her rape… or anything else'. Cecily appeared in court to make formal acknowledgement of this document, which is also witnessed by a prestigious list of names already familiar to us as associates of Chaucer. Sir William Beauchamp, chamberlain of the King's household, returns Chaucer's favour of 1378 when Chaucer stood surety for him. The names of Sir John Clanvowe and Sir William Neville, knights of the King's chamber, are recorded alongside those of Richard Morel and John Philipot, former Mayor of London and, as collector of customs, Chaucer's boss during his time as controller.

Geoffrey Chaucer was no stranger to the law. One of the most famous legal clashes of Chaucer's time was the case of Sir Richard Scrope versus his cousin Sir Robert Grosvenor, heard on 15th October 1386. Their dispute had in fact begun some time in 1385 and it dragged on for many years until it was resolved in Scrope's favour in 1390. Chaucer tells the court how he was sent on a military expedition to Rethel, near Reims in France. During this time he saw Sir Richard wearing the coat of arms in question; everyone knew, he said, that these were the Scrope family arms of old. Back home in London, Chaucer was in Friday Street when he spotted a new sign outside a particular shop. The sign was decorated with the Scrope coat of arms. He asked who had hung them there and was told they belonged to a knight from Cheshire called Robert Grosvenor. Chaucer declared that this was news to him. The record of this trial testifies to Chaucer's social standing, for he appears in the documents – and not for the first time – alongside eminent society figures and personal friends like Sir John Clanvowe, Sir Peter Bukton and Sir Lewis Clifford, all of whom acted as witnesses in the same trial.

Chaucer's name appears in other extant documents from the late 1370s onwards when he was guarantor in a number of cases, all for important figures or for men whom he knew personally. He was surety for a fellow former esquire John de Romsey in 1375 when that same John Romsey was treasurer of Calais. A few years later in 1378, Chaucer and another esquire named John Beverley acted as mainprize when Sir William Beauchamp was made custodian of Pembroke Castle. Beauchamp was later to hold the key post of chamberlain of the royal household. He also assisted Chaucer on one of his diplomatic missions to Calais in 1387. In 1381 Chaucer was one of several guarantors for John Hend, who was later Mayor of London and an important financial backer of Richard II's court. In January 1386 during his sojourn in Kent, Chaucer was present at the Court of Common Pleas to stand surety for his brother-in-law Simon Manning. More generally, records show that Chaucer regularly sold his services as guarantor in a number of cases during the years of 1387 and 1388.

Without doubt instances such as these belong to that wider social and economic web to which Chaucer belonged. In November 1375, for instance, he was granted the wardship of Edmund Staplegate and in the following month that of William Soles. Wards of court were traditionally heirs of the King's chief tenants. Wardships were frequently sold or granted by the King to his particular favourites and were potentially lucrative businesses. A ward's property might be invested for the personal use of the one holding the wardship or payment demanded when the ward came of age and married. Chaucer certainly does this with Staplegate, for when Edmund married we know that he had to buy back his marriage payment from Chaucer for the phenomenal sum of £104. Once more Chaucer was able to profit from royal favour and advantageous legal and social conditions.

There is no doubt that the late medieval age was exceptionally litigious. Chaucer's visibility in the legal archives is evidence of his high profile as a public servant and the invidious workings of a world based on preferment and favouritism. Yet Chaucer, like many others, was not immune from prosecution himself. In 1379 Chaucer appointed an attorney to defend him from accusations of 'contempt and trespass'. The case was brought by a Thomas Stondon and was clearly a serious charge as it was to be heard before the King's Bench. There is no record of it arriving there so, presumably, the case was dropped or, as was common in those times, settled out of court. The Champain versus Chaucer case was a more complex affair altogether.

Three other associated documents survive alongside Cecily Champain's release of Chaucer from the charge of rape. These are all enrolled in the court of the Mayor and Alderman of London, a lesser court than the Chancery of the original rape accusation. On 28th June 1380 two citizens of London – Richard Goodchild, cutler, and John Grove, armourer – release the said Geoffrey Chaucer 'from all actions of law they might have against him'. Another document of the same date offers a similar release but this one is made by Cecily, who releases not Chaucer but Goodchild and Grove. The plot thickens when on 2nd July 1380 Grove acknowledges, and later pays, a large debt of £10 owed to Cecily Champain. Here a humble armourer pays a sum so large that it comprises more than half of Chaucer's annual salary for his customs posts. At roughly the same time Chaucer seemingly calls in a number of personal debts. On 28th November he collects the half-yearly instalments on his two royal annuities plus £14 in expenses for his mission to Lombardy, that is for a trip made two years earlier in 1378 and not called in until now. On 6th March 1381 Chaucer receives £22 in compensation for expenses owed since 1377 on a number of journeys made to France on the King's behalf. Finally, on 19th June 1381, Chaucer sells the house on Thames Street that he had inherited from his mother.

Were these events merely coincidental, completely unconnected occurrences, or are they evidence of something far more damaging that Chaucer – and his friends – needed urgently to resolve? The medieval legal term *'raptus'* varied in meaning. Most often it referred to abduction. This was usually intended to secure an inheritance – as was the case when Chaucer's father was abducted by his aunt – or for other financial gain. In such instances the crime was recorded as *'raptus et abduxerunt'* (raped and abducted) to distinguish it from its other meaning, which is rape as we would understand it today. Legal documents marked this in a different way, usually by the suffix *'violavit'* (violated) or *'defloravit'* (deflowered), or even *'afforciavit contra voluntatem'* (unwillingly forced). Not a single one of any of these possibilities appears on Chaucer's file. The absence of the specific and lesser charge of *'et abduxerunt'* almost always indicates that this was a forced sexual crime and, so, I think that the charge against Chaucer must have been a serious one. Yet what are we to make of this wording or that odd release of 'or anything else' on the original document?

Many scholars ignore this event altogether or else gloss it as a minor comedy of errors in which Chaucer was simply acting on behalf of another, as some did in those times, and so is erroneously charged in the fall-out. Yet the presence and authoritative weight of Chaucer's inner circle of friends indicates the severity of the case and certainly proves that Chaucer was keen to have all charges dropped. Similarly, both the alacrity with which he called in long-standing debts and the large sums of money involved suggests a buy-off of some kind. The mention of these unknowns, Goodchild and Grove, plus Grove's payment to Cecily for reasons unspecified and then their sudden disappearance from all further documents, points to the distinct possibility that they were acting as intermediaries on behalf of Chaucer – who subsequently compensated Cecily off the record. So, did Chaucer rape her and buy her silence? Or was the accusation a bluff in which she threatened rape in order to demand a significant financial remuneration for some reason?

One suggestion is that Chaucer and Cecily Champain had a relationship that ended acrimoniously. Others write a love-child into that scenario, a possibility that the respected biographer and academic Derek Pearsall dismisses as 'circumstantial and not proven'. Nothing in the records nails the case either way, but nor would it if Chaucer wanted to ensure nothing was left to incriminate him. It seems that someone took steps to keep the case, whatever that might have been, out of court. In witnessing Cecily's release, Chaucer's friends assured that he was free from prosecution; their presence does *not* guarantee that there was no case to answer. It is also clear that Cecily Champain must have been known to Chaucer, probably personally. Chaucer was acquainted with Alice Perrers, mistress of Edward III and in long service to Edward's wife as a lady of the chamber, just like Chaucer's wife Philippa. Alice Perrers was friends with Richard Lyons who, in turn, was close to Chaucer's father John and Chaucer's superior at the customs when he started there as controller. Adam de Bury, the Mayor of London who granted the lease on Chaucer's grace-and-favour Aldgate house, was a member of the same circle. And Alice Perrers was Cecily's stepmother.

The circumstantial evidence is certainly convincing. Here is Chaucer, a man in his forties with a base in Aldgate, his wife in Lincoln with her sister, with whom she resides for some eight years. Here is Cecily, a woman in her twenties and hence too old for the usual 'rape and abduction' scenario. Here is the mysterious dedication of Chaucer's *Treatise on the Astrolabe* made to 'my litel sone' Lewis. Are we to infer from this that

Chaucer had not one but two boys? The Lewis in question would be eleven years old in 1391 according to this reference. It makes the date of his conception around 1380, the year in which Cecily releases Chaucer from all charges of rape and when he begins to make a series of financial arrangements that may well signpost a commitment to an illegitimate son and his mother. Lewis reliably appears just once more in the records. A document from Carmarthen Castle in Wales, dated 1403, mentions Thomas Chaucer and 'Ludowicus Chaucer', citing them both as men-of-arms. Lewis may, of course, have been a late baby for Philippa. Somehow, I think not.

Danger at Court
1385–90

Late medieval England was an increasingly fractious net of inter-connection and obligation. The roots of its dangerous dynamics of power lay deep in the Ricardian court. Richard was interested in meritocracy rather than birthright. He wanted to appoint his own peers, those who were clever or useful but not men of rank. For instance, he appointed Michael de la Pole, a merchant's son, as his Chancellor of the Realm and later made him Earl of Suffolk, while his chamber knight John Beauchamp became Baron of Kidderminster. As Richard II approached his majority he began to assert his independence from those advisors and relations who had effectively governed for him.

The most powerful of these was a group known as the Lords Appellant. It included men like Richard Fitzalan, Earl of Arundel; Thomas Beauchamp, Earl of Warwick; Thomas Mowbray, Earl of Nottingham; Thomas Woodstock, Duke of Gloucester; and John of Gaunt's son Henry Bolingbroke, who was later crowned Henry IV. Some of these were also Richard's uncles, seeking to maintain their traditional rights and angered by Richard's rejection of them in favour of his own men. More generally, this powerful group of lords sought to control Richard II's fiscal and administrative policies and to reform a court built – or so they maintained – on the principles of cronyism. The problem for Geoffrey Chaucer was that he was associated with both the Lancastrians and Lords Appellant – via John of Gaunt *and* the King's inner circle.

It is surely not coincidence that at this point in his life Chaucer was increasingly absent from the city of London. In 1385 he became a Justice of the Peace for Kent, a position renewed the following year and probably retained up until 12th July 1389. At the same time as Chaucer acted as a JP, he was also a Member of Parliament. Though Chaucer was never knighted, he was clearly sufficiently esteemed to be rewarded as an elected knight of the shire. As such, he received the same pay as a knight on active service abroad for all the days when Parliament was in session. To the best of our knowledge Chaucer sat in only one Parliament, the so-called 'Wonderful Parliament' which ran from 1st October to 28th November 1386. Historians and academics have long speculated about the reason for Chaucer's presence at a session significant for its attack on the King's choice of advisors. Was Chaucer working on behalf of the King, as someone whose proven diplomatic skills might defuse tensions and safeguard the passage of more difficult bills or memos? Chaucer was undoubtedly still in royal service at this time and close to a number of those who suffered the consequences of actions taken against Richard and his favourites.

In 1387 the Lords Appellant successfully impeached the royal chancellor and made Richard subject to a governing commission – effectively a committee of protection ensuring that he all but lost his mandate to rule. They also brought charges of treason against some of Richard's circle, including Chaucer's associate Simon Burley, Richard's beloved tutor, and Sir Robert Tresilian who was the Chief Justice of the King's Bench at the same time as Chaucer was a JP. Both Burley and Tresilian were later executed, as was another of Chaucer's known acquaintances, the eminent merchant and former Mayor of London Sir Nicholas Brembre. The Lords Appellant used this same Parliament to undermine Richard's bureaucratic control by petitioning against the appointment of certain offices that they believed to be susceptible to abuse. Their primary target was the controllers of customs, a job usually granted for life. The

Lords demanded the removal of all those currently in post and barred all future contracts of this kind.

Chaucer's sole experience of sitting in Parliament in that 1386 session must have been an uncomfortable one. A number of his associates lost their jobs and, in some cases, their heads. Although Chaucer's controllerships of the wool and petty customs were not offices of the kind the Lords Appellant protested about, and although the petition in fact came to nothing at this time, it cannot be coincidence that Chaucer resigned both positions shortly afterwards and moved out of London. Within a week of the dissolution of Parliament Adam Yardley became Chaucer's successor at the wool custom. Henry Gisors soon followed at the petty custom.

A few years later in the 'Merciless Parliament' of 1388, the Lords Appellant prosecuted their grievances more vigorously and soon controlled medieval England. More of the King's friends and close advisors were removed from office, exiled or sentenced to death after the Lords successfully petitioned against the royal practice of rewarding favour with life annuities. Those annuities that were granted by Edward III and then renewed or added to by Richard II were particularly closely scrutinised. Chaucer had, of course, been favoured in this way by both kings – Edward in 1367 and more recently by Richard. The Appellants condemned eleven of Richard's retainers in all; Chaucer had known contact with at least eight of them. Some of Chaucer's close friends – Richard's chamber knights Sir Lewis Clifford, John Clanvowe, William Neville, Richard Stury and Philip de la Vache – survived but quickly distanced themselves from the Ricardian court. His position compromised, Chaucer began to follow suit. His controllerships had already gone. By 1st May 1388 Geoffrey Chaucer had sold his annuities to one John Scalby.

Yet he remained in the King's service. In the summer of the previous year, he had travelled to Calais on royal business accompanied by Sir William Beauchamp. Like many others, Chaucer received letters of protection for this trip, but it seems that only

Chaucer and Beauchamp actually made the journey. The nature of his business goes unrecorded. Was this a bona fide assignment or was it simply to keep him out of sight and harm in these troubled times? Chaucer is also noted in four separate legal cases at the Court of Common Pleas during this time. Most sureties were settled out of court but Chaucer was summoned to appear in all of them. An arrest warrant was issued for one and a final warning to appear for another. He failed to turn up for a single one of them. Were these ruses to flush Chaucer out of Kent where he had increasingly made his home? Chaucer was certainly the type of professional courtier that the Appellants wished to target and part of the same royal faction at odds with the barons. He disappears from the records around the time that Richard II is temporarily deposed.

In the closing years of the 1380s Richard finally came of age. In 1389 he sought to resume his kingship, an enterprise in which he was aided by two pieces of luck. The Appellant knights were weakened after their unsuccessful forays against the French and their invasion of Scotland in 1388. Then John of Gaunt returned from manoeuvres in Spain and Bordeaux to give Richard the military and psychological strength he needed to face down his accusers. Geoffrey Chaucer returned to the royal fold when Richard II made him Clerk of the King's Works in the July of 1389, just a few months after he resumed his crown.

It is possible that Chaucer was also steward of the royal palaces in Kent, Eltham and maybe Sheen for the position of clerk was fairly arduous. It did though have an excellent salary and came with a wealth of social and political opportunities. The clerk was project-manager for all royal construction and repair work. Together with his assistant, Chaucer was responsible for overseeing building and maintenance plans, organising workers – many of them highly respected master builders or eminent traders – and ordering all materials. He was also in charge of all financial transactions – administering a budget, paying wages and collecting loans. We know that during his time as Clerk of the King's Works Chaucer was closely involved in a project at the Tower of London where the King wanted to build a new wharf, and also that he supervised the erection of the lists for the famous Smithfield Tournament of 1390. Another of Chaucer's commissions was to oversee repairs to drainage ditches and banks along the Thames between Greenwich and Woolwich after the great storm of March 1390. Coincidentally this brought him into renewed contact with Richard Stury, with whom Chaucer was ransomed in the French campaign of 1359–60 and who accompanied him to treat for peace with France in 1377. Geoffrey Chaucer was back in London and once again visibly allied to the Ricardian court.

Keys to Remembrance

'... if that olde bokes weren aweye [gone]
Yloren [lost] were of remembraunce the keye.'
The Legend of Good Women, G Prologue, 25–6

When the Host of *The Canterbury Tales* calls upon Chaucer
the pilgrim-narrator to recount a merry tale he was surely not
expecting 'The Tale of Sir Thopas'. Chaucer reluctantly offers
the only thing he knows, or so he says, a rhyme learned long ago
and truly the best he has. Harry Bailly is anticipating a dainty
piece of verse fit for the self-effacing little chap of Chaucer's
apparent self-portrait. Instead, the company is bludgeoned with
a literary in-joke, a romance complete with jog-trot rhythm and
a ludicrous coming-of-age encounter with Sir Elephant. The
Host is so outraged by this 'rym doggerel' that he cuts Chaucer
off in mid-sentence to tell him that his 'drasty rymyng is nat
worth a toord!'.

Chaucer's presentation of himself as the unlearned and
somewhat absurd narrator of what is undoubtedly some of the
finest poetry in the English language in *The Canterbury Tales*, if
nowhere else, is patently a tongue-in-cheek bluff. Yet it resembles
the 'Chaucer' self-penned elsewhere: the inexperienced bookworm of *The Book of the Duchess* reading romances throughout
the endless nights of his eight-year-long insomnia; and the
slow-witted poet of *The House of Fame*, *The Parliament of Fowls*,

Troilus and Criseyde and *The Legend of Good Women*, that man standing on the sidelines and writing of the most powerful human emotions 'for al be that I knowe nat Love in dede' (*The Parliament of Fowls*). In part, too, Chaucer's seemingly bewildered narrators are *careful* tellers consciously negotiating a minefield of social and literary change. Theirs is the courteous, self-effacing voice of the court-poet, inferior in rank to most of his audience, no longer a professional minstrel-player declaiming his performance skills but an aspiring courtier who also happens to write poetry.

However tempting it might be to seek correspondences, there is undoubtedly a world of difference between a first-person narrator and an author, especially when the author in question is as elusive as Geoffrey Chaucer. The complex material production of medieval writing further detracts from any potential parallels between the two, for this was an age that neither prized originality nor grasped the notion of copyright or sole authorship rights. Stories were recycled and retold with reference to their sources in a process known as '*auctoritas*', which seemingly valued other authors of a tale more highly than the one currently writing. Scribes copied and circulated an author's manuscript, sometimes complete with mistakes, deliberate omissions or alterations. Audiences glossed and annotated manuscripts and generally demanded bespoke versions in keeping with their own tastes and inclinations regardless of authorial intent. So in the short poem 'Chaucers Wordes Unto Adam, His Owne Scriveyn', Chaucer berates his scribe for a negligence that too often results in the physical destruction of a manuscript – caused by rubbing out and scraping the parchment – and also Adam's failure to reproduce Chaucer's words exactly or copy 'trewe'.

Yet late medieval literary culture was at a crossroads, caught up in an emerging print transmission of literature whose claims were rather different from what had so far stood the test of time. Work began to be printed rather than simply repeatedly transcribed so that texts became more stable and less vulnerable to interference. People were also just beginning to be aware of what we would recognise as the 'self' or subjectivity; hence, the popular device of first-person narration was ever more flexible and problematic. So, too, notions about authorship took on new meaning. Once, most literary works were produced anonymously. Even where a text was signed, the name was rarely a clue to the identity of its writer; it might be a scribal attribution or even a fake claim, something attached to other known or clearly authored works as part of a miscellaneous collection, or perhaps even in an effort to sell the work. Chaucer's writing was particularly susceptible to the latter with an incredible fifty-one works spuriously claimed as his.

Chaucer seems to have been acutely conscious of the impact of an author's name. Here he was no doubt influenced by Italian and French poets or the poetic vision of a man like Dante, whom he wished to emulate. Print also allowed work to be signed more readily than oral transmission of texts. Chaucer readily self-attributes a number of his poems. In so doing, he signals less about Chaucer the man and much more about how he sought to position himself as a serious writer. The medieval term 'auctour' was a privileged one, with a special authority usually reserved for the classical writers of Greece and Rome. Alternatively a 'compiler' gathered up work without adding anything to it. Chaucer describes himself as a compiler in *A Treatise on the Astrolabe*. Elsewhere he calls himself a translator or a 'makere'. Both references are surely disingenuous, more designed to point up some of the issues associated with medieval authorship than accurate definitions of his work.

On the one hand, Chaucer – or rather his narrators – claims to follow his sources with the utmost care and fidelity, arguing that old books are the key to remembrance, as, for example, in the F Prologue to *The Legend of Good Women*:

Than mote we to bokes that we fynde,
Thurgh whiche that olde thinges ben in mynde,
And to the doctrine of these olde wyse,
Yeve credence, in every skilful wise,
That tellen of these olde approved stories
Of holynesse, of regnes, of victories,
Of love, of hate, of other sundry thynges,
Of whiche I may not maken rehersynges.
And yf that olde bokes were aweye,
Yloren were of remembraunce the keye.
Wel ought us thane honouren and beleve
These bokes, there we han noon other preve.
    And as for me, though that I konne but lyte,
On bokes for to rede I me delyte…

… and insisting, as in *Troilus and Criseyde*, that 'For as myn auctour seyde, so sey I'. He identifies himself as a translator in *The Canterbury Tales* when he insists in the 'General Prologue' on reporting what he has heard word for word rather than telling a tale 'untrewe', even if it offends. Otherwise he would be inventing things or telling his tale falsely. The idea that Chaucer merely replicates the content of other works is also the comic excuse that Alceste offers the God of Love when he castigates Chaucer-the-narrator for writing only ill of women in the *Legend*. Alceste declares that Chaucer cannot be held responsible for what he writes for he is but a rather stupid translator who takes little notice of the material he copies.

Yet despite the protestations of his narrators, Chaucer's 'makyng' means that he continually challenges, rather than simply follows, his authoritative source material to offer fresh perspectives on old stories. The work that succeeds *Troilus and Criseyde* is *The Legend of Good Women*. In part, this poem is a self-reflexive gesture that serves not only to establish Chaucer's authorship of *Troilus* – which is the poem the God of Love is particularly irked by – but also as a dialogue about writing, when the narrator of the

Legend is forced into the reductive and ultimately aborted task of writing only of good women as penance for his earlier sins.

Chaucer's naive narrators consistently allow the man to slip from view, even as the poet stakes a claim for posterity. At the close of *Troilus and Criseyde*, Chaucer sends his 'litel bok' out into the ether with the command that it be subject to all poetry, that it venerates – 'kisses' – the steps where others have passed before him: Virgil, Ovid, Homer, Lucan, Statius, those great and properly recognised *authors*. Here he implicitly makes himself next in line and so aligns himself with the idea of the 'sixth of the six' seen in Dante's *Divine Comedy* and in poets like Boccaccio who use it to secure a reputation as a serious artist. Also in *Troilus and Criseyde*, Chaucer places himself in a web of writers, past and present, with his commendation to his friends 'moral Gower' and 'philosophical Strode'. In the same way, Chaucer seeks to mark a literary vernacular tradition by listing his own works: in the *Legend*'s Prologue where he is represented as one who translated *The Romance of the Rose* and *Troilus and Criseyde*, as well as a number of courtly poems in the service of love; in 'The Man of Law's Tale', cited as the author of *The Book of the Duchess* and *The Legend of Good Women*; and the definitive list of his works offered in the 'Retraction'.

These Chaucer-narrators are rather more than literary conceits, however. They permit Chaucer to explore the vexed issue of vernacular authorship that was so pertinent to the political landscape of late medieval culture. Medieval writings in English were few and far between. Some, like Chaucer's friend John Gower and the *Piers Plowman* poet William Langland, had begun to pen works in their mother tongue. Chaucer was the first to write exclusively in English at a time when French, the tongue of the Anglo-Norman descendants of the 1066 conquerors, was still the official language of England. While Wyclif was fomenting dissent by insisting that Bibles ought to be written in English, not Latin, for all to understand, Chaucer was making a potentially dangerous statement of his own.

Art and Life

Audiences – popular and scholarly alike – persist in their search for a Chaucer who will be found deep in the corners of his own fictional trickery. The *Tales* is particularly susceptible to illusory revelations of this kind. It has a first-person narrator who claims to report an actual event, a pilgrimage plotted along the co-ordinates of a familiar route and measured by reference to real places and the times of a medieval holy day. Its characters are defined by occupation and 'estate' or social class. Those knights, pardoners, friars and franklins inhabit Chaucer's *now* with its upheavals, discontents and displacement of old-style feudal allegiances, even as their history is a fabricated, outmoded classical or pagan past, or else an idyllic, legendary Arthurian point of origin. Real life scarcely intrudes or does so obliquely with a nod to Jack Straw, the rebel leader of the 1381 Peasants' Revolt, or the stench of a Lollard in the wind.

The apparent verisimilitude of *The Canterbury Tales* seduces us into believing that the man could speak through his art. But in whose voice do we hear him? Chaucer, the pilgrim-narrator's? The Miller's? Chauntecleer's, the rooster in 'The Nun's Priest's Tale'? And is this 'man' consistent in other writings? Is the dreamy introvert of *The House of Fame* the same half-comic persona who critiques late medieval culture but ensures that Chaucer-the-author cannot be held accountable, or at least not until he is made to retract everything at the end of the *Tales*?

Does 'Chaucer' speak as that detached, morally ambiguous ironist beloved of much academic criticism and found, according to E. Talbot Donaldson in his book *Speaking of Chaucer* (1970), in the gap between the man and his elvish, enigmatic mouthpiece?

In 1868, even as F.J. Furnivall was offering a renewed focus on Chaucer's literature by establishing the Chaucer Society, he – among countless others – was still insisting that art and life are inextricably allied, that we must 'start with him in his sorrow, walk with him through it into the fresh sunshine of his later life, and then down to the chill and poverty of his old age'. Peter Ackroyd's biography (2004) typically refuses to engage with Chaucer's poems as works of literature. Instead, all those convincing details that inject colour and vigour into Chaucer's material are read as revelation, as clues to a reality that impacts upon the man. There are undoubtedly real-life references in Chaucer's work. Herry Bailey, a well-known Southwark landlord, was probably the basis for Chaucer's Host Harry Bailly in *The Canterbury Tales*. Chaucer's cheating Cook, Roger of Ware, existed, as did his Shipman, known to Chaucer via a dispute he mediated in August 1373 between a Genoese ship owner, John de Nigris, and the Dartmouth port authorities who inexplicably impounded his ship. The Sergeant-at-Law of the 'General Prologue' may have had a real-life counterpart known as Thomas Pynchbeck, while a comment on one 'Colle tregetour' in *The House of Fame* – a conjuror whose best trick is hiding a windmill under a walnut shell – probably referred to the famous magician Colin of England.

To a large extent, most of these are simply the kinds of details all writers have in their repertoire. But other covert and more explicit references to Richard or his court deeply implicate Chaucer in the political context of his time. Perhaps the clearest indication of life meeting art is in Chaucer's *Book of the Duchess*, but even here many misread the nature of the dedication. The poem was written as a memorial for John of Gaunt's first wife

Blanche, Duchess of Lancaster, some twelve months after her death, reputedly from plague. The commission does not mean that Gaunt was Chaucer's patron, as is commonly assumed. Rather, the commission may have come both through Chaucer's increasing poetic reputation and his family connection to the recipient. Equally, the intent of the entire commemoration may well have been to stake a political claim by reminding everyone of Gaunt's Lancastrian power base and connection to the English Crown. Accordingly, the poem emblematises a series of Lancastrian references. The virtuous Lady, object of the man-in-black's affection, is called 'goode faire White' in keeping with devotion to the meaning of her name 'Blanche'. Her melancholy lover rides off at the end, back to a white-walled castle said to be 'by saint John, on a rich hill': in other words, John, Earl of Richmond and Duke of Lancaster, which became Gaunt's full title when he married Blanche. Chaucer later attributes the poem more directly when the narrator of *The Legend of Good Women* tells of having written 'The Death of the Duchess Blanche'.

We think *The Parliament of Fowls* is dedicated to Anne of Bohemia, who married Richard II. At that time she had two other suitors for her hand, Charles of France and Friedrich of Messieu. Along with Richard, they become the three eagles who compete for the favour of the female tercel in Chaucer's poem. *The Legend of Good Women* is similarly offered to Richard's queen, here represented by the graceful and cultured Alceste, queen of the daisies. Alceste's appreciation of the narrator's artistic endeavours certainly corresponds to Anne's known patronage of literature. Scholars have long puzzled over the existence of two Prologues to the *Legend*, neither of them complete. Many believe that the later G Prologue excises all references to Anne of Bohemia after her death in 1394, when Richard was reputedly so distressed that he destroyed her manor house at Sheen. Certainly only the G version makes reference to the lily or fleur-de-lis that was associated with Richard's subsequent wife Isabella of France.

'Lak of Stedfastnesse' used to be thought of as a coded reprimand to a tyrannical king who was about to be usurped. We now believe that this is in fact an earlier piece, written in the years 1389–90 and not at the end of Richard's reign. In this context, the speaker's advice to be honourable, care for those close to you and punish wrongdoers is not criticism but, in the words of Terry Jones, 'little more than a policy statement on behalf of the king'. 'The Tale of Melibee' may be a similar attempt at advocacy, with its advice to princes and its rehearsal of some major debates about the nature of kingship and power. The writing of 'Lak of Stedfastnesse' coincides too with Chaucer's appointment as the Clerk of the King's Works, Richard's reward for Geoffrey's faith in the years of the Appellant rule. Chaucer held this post for just two years. What happened to make him relinquish it?

Last Acts
1391–1400

By 17th June 1391 the Clerk of the King's Works was one John Gedney and not Geoffrey Chaucer. On 3rd September of the previous year Chaucer had been robbed of a large sum of money – plus his horse – while on his travels overseeing building works. The same happened three days later when he was the target of thieves twice in one day. It was presumably well known that Chaucer often carried money, while the peripatetic nature of his employment also made him vulnerable to attack. Yet none of this prompted the loss of his job. Chaucer was, in fact, dismissed for fraud.

The audit of 1391 allegedly uncovered a massive overspend in Chaucer's accounts. It occurred because of a single outstanding debt owed by Sir William Thorpe and credited as paid when it had not been – except that Chaucer *had* actually balanced the books by paying for this himself. The Crown clearly accepted this fact, for it repaid the huge amount of £66 to Chaucer in a series of quarterly instalments, the last dated 13th July 1392. Nevertheless, Chaucer was asked to step down from his position. Just after Chaucer received the final instalment on the 'Thorpe' loan, a moneylender called William Venour repeatedly tried to call in a small debt. We do not know if the business at the Clerk's office left Chaucer in financial difficulty or if this is evidence of further irregularity in his monetary affairs. What we do know is that this was only the first of a series of inexplicable transactions that took place throughout the '90s.

Chaucer was pursued through the courts again in 1394. He settled out of court on exactly the same day as he took an advance payment on the next instalment of the annuity (for £20) Richard had given him in the February of that same year. He was summonsed again in 1398 for another large sum: £14. This time the case was serious enough for Chaucer to hire an attorney to guarantee against arrest while he was abroad on King's business. The issue of protection is not unusual in itself but this particular warrant was valid for two whole years and specifically protected Chaucer against all lawsuits for that period of time. Was the royal permit issued because of the gravity of this particular legal action? Or does it signify that something potentially more worrying was afoot?

The political climate of 1398 onwards was marked by faction-making and the settling of old scores. Henry Bolingbroke and Richard II were cousins and childhood friends. When Henry and their cousin Thomas Mowbray quarrelled, Richard tried to mediate but was unsuccessful. The dispute was apparently serious enough to warrant a duel to the death. Richard agreed to oversee the joust but just as it was about to start he stopped it. Later in the day he exiled Mowbray for life and banished Henry to France – with the whopping sum of £2,000 a year for the period of his exile. Many believe that Richard intended to recall Henry after a short time but events came to a head before he could do so. Henry's father John of Gaunt died in 1399. Instead of allowing Henry to claim his inheritance as he had already promised, Richard told Henry that he was holding the estate until either he or his son sued him for it.

Thomas Arundel, the former Archbishop of Canterbury, had also been exiled by Richard. Arundel was the youngest brother of Richard Fitzalan, Earl of Arundel, who had been a leading player in the 1388–9 rebellion against Richard by the Lords Appellant. Thomas had not forgotten how the King had tricked him into persuading Fitzalan to come out of hiding only to have him executed. By January 1398 Richard had given Arundel's considerable estate from the Church to his new Archbishop; clearly he had no plans to recall Arundel at any time. We know that Henry and Arundel broke the rules of their exile – which had forbidden all contact – and met in Paris some time before 1399. The deposition of Richard was both unexpected and swift. While an unsuspecting Richard sailed to Ireland, Bolingbroke was back in the north of England looking to gather an army. Richard was forced to abdicate at the end of September 1399. Henry Bolingbroke, Earl of Derby, was crowned Henry IV a couple of weeks later.

Chaucer was also indirectly affected by these events. Once he had lost the clerkship Chaucer had only his annuities to rely on and, presumably, his pay from the position as deputy forester for North Petherton, Somerset, a job he was given in 1390 and about which we know nothing (except that it was later also held by his son). When Gaunt died, others – including Thomas Chaucer – tried to secure the continuation of their pensions when Richard confiscated Gaunt's estate. Chaucer did not. It seems that, once more, he was standing aside at this difficult time and waiting to see how things panned out. Once Henry was crowned he immediately confirmed Chaucer's previous pension from Richard and even added one of his own for forty marks a year. Yet he rarely paid them.

Writing from the refuge of the abbey house, Chaucer penned 'The Complaint of Chaucer to his Purse' to petition Henry for money. Henry authorised payment of the November 1399 instalment; it never arrived. The situation seemed more promising when on 21st February 1400 the King gave Chaucer a present of £10. A few months later he issued a mandate to expedite the payment of all arrears owed to Chaucer and backdated this to the start of his reign. Only two payments were ever made, and these were part payments of Chaucer's annuities from Richard and Edward III (plus the yearly tun of wine granted by Richard in 1397). Nothing was forthcoming from Henry IV, who seems almost to have gone out of his way to ensure that Chaucer's financial lifeline was cut.

The two payments that Chaucer did receive during this time – on 21st February and 5th June 1400 – he did not collect in person, as was usually the case. Was he ill, or, as the evidence seems to suggest, was he eager to avoid Henry IV and his followers? By the autumn of that year Chaucer had vanished without trace from all historical records.

Lodestars and Legends

England, 20th April 1940. It is more than five hundred years since Chaucer's death. The Second World War is in full swing and, faced with a threat to national security, that bastion of nationhood the broadsheet newspaper *The Times* runs an editorial in its Literary Supplement entitled 'Chaucer's England!'. It begins, 'No man in history is more essentially English than Chaucer'. A short while earlier, in his seminal book *Chaucer* (1932), G.K. Chesterton had reclaimed Geoffrey Chaucer as the founding father not only of English poetry – a term originally coined by the dramatist John Dryden in the Preface to his own *Fables* back in 1700 – but as the father of 'his Country'.

The conviction that through his work we access a Chaucer who embodies everything we understand by 'nation' or 'Englishness' was at its height in the Victorian age and during the world wars of the twentieth century. In his two-volume book entitled *Chaucer's England* (1869), Matthew Browne describes an Englishman as one who creates a community. He may be a missionary, a colonial explorer or something less dramatic, but he will have, above all else, a yearning *to bring together*. Browne argued that Chaucer possessed this quality in abundance. We see it through the direct language, fellowship and social enterprise of *The Canterbury Tales* that, according to Browne, encapsulates this essential 'Englishness'. Matthew Browne is certainly not atypical in making this claim for Chaucer. The poet and critic

Steve Ellis notes a Victorian tendency to dismiss Continental influences on Chaucer's work in favour of the everyday domesticity of a poem like the *Tales*, which quickly became emblematic of a so-called 'national spirit'.

John Richard Green's *A Short History of the English People*, published in 1916, exemplifies the persistence of this idea. Green remarks that the 'genius of Chaucer' is that he is 'English to the core'. This 'Englishness' constitutes a number of features, all allegedly readily extrapolated from Chaucer's poetry and subsequently imposed on an author and a man – the two become indistinguishable – who is made to stand for a particular, usually conservative, set of cultural values. This enterprise is often a nostalgic one, a search for a 'Golden Age' that contemporaneous society has somehow lost sight of. In his Introduction to P.J. Harvey Darton's *Tales of the Canterbury Pilgrims: Retold From Chaucer and Others* (1904), F.J. Furnivall writes that Chaucer 'handed us down the England and the language which we possess'. Chesterton summarises Chaucer thus: 'He minds his own business;... is rather silent and yet somehow sociable... he is manly; he is modest... solid and reasonable and reliable... generally fond of a joke.' This same genial, self-effacing and upstanding citizen is also an orthodox Catholic, apparently, 'the last great Englishman of a united Christendom' in whom the mundane becomes mythical, 'an emblem of England... as large as the land and as old as the nation'.

Chaucer's decision to write in vernacular English and make 'a national language', to use Chesterton's terminology, is one of the sparks for a tradition that depicts him as not only a literary forefather but a patriot who, again according to Chesterton, 'came very near to making a nation'. The concrete details of everyday life seen in, say, *The Canterbury Tales*, might construct Chaucer-the-ordinary-man, but what of the mordant social commentary of the same poem, Chaucer's alleged Lollard sympathies or the man reputed in the sixteenth century for the breadth of his learning, one whom the scholar Hoccleve, cited in

Brewer's *Chaucer, The Critical Heritage* (1978), calls a 'universal father in science', greater even than Aristotle in philosophy and all written 'in our tonge'? How do we account for the dream-vision poems, his lost lays and love songs, or the fact that Chaucer's 'true' English voice flourished in a literary and cultural context that was, above all, French and Italian?

Despite this, the same old images of Chaucer recur. Peter Ackroyd's biography compares Chaucer to Shakespeare in that 'His was a thoroughly native genius'. In so doing he imposes modern ideas about what constitutes a nation upon a not necessarily compatible medieval grasp of the term. To call Geoffrey Chaucer the 'father of *English* poetry' presupposes an identity he could never have, in reality, possessed. The medieval term 'nacioun' encompassed notions of birth, family and lineage rather than a specifically unified, sovereign or political reality. Equally, 'kingship' and 'nationhood' were not synonymous in medieval culture. England had been a colonised nation since 1066. The official language of the English court was French. English kings pressed their rights to the French Crown even as their parliaments began to be conducted in English and, certainly by 1362, English was permissible in courts of law. Terms such as 'English' or 'England' invoked a series of competing, contingent and precarious allegiances that make nonsense of the nationhood Chaucer is made to emblematise.

Those who speak more specifically of Chaucer's engendering in poetry are perhaps on surer ground. Chaucer is presented as a father-figure for a literary vernacular right from the immediate years after his death and in spite of the provisional nature of that construction. His great friend John Gower has the figure of Venus greet 'Chaucer' as 'mi disciple and mi poet' in his *Confessio Amantis* and so returns the favour of the reference to 'moral Gower' in Chaucer's *Troilus and Criseyde*. In the fifteenth-century *Testament of Love*, Thomas Usk's Cupid describes Chaucer as 'the noble philosophical poete in Englissh'. Hoccleve and Lydgate both esteem him as an inspirational 'father' and translator. John

Lydgate writes of him in the *Fall of Princes* as one 'whom al this land sholde off right preferred,/ Sith off our language he was the lode sterre'. The notion of Chaucer as a guide to others or a linguistic vantage point is replicated in Caxton's Epilogue to Chaucer's translation (from Latin) of Boethius. Caxton commends him as 'the worshipful fader & first foundeur & enbelissher of ornate eloquence in our englissh'. Of course, those same writers who laud Chaucer's literary innovations and configure him as an originary point for English poetry, also enhance their own reputations along the way, just as Chaucer did with those French and Italian greats before him. And from this celebration – part truth, part propaganda – Chaucer's legend is well and truly born.

Facts and Fictions

No manuscript actually written by Chaucer survives from his lifetime. When other writers were beginning to gather up their literary efforts and to publish their collected works, Chaucer apparently left no authorial copy behind. It remains to others, those poets, compilers and publishers of the fifteenth century and beyond, to collate Chaucer's poetry according to their own enterprise and vested interests. Some believe that an author's literary legacy reveals at least something of the person writing it. In turn, a definitive list of publications helps to shape our responses to that author and their work. Those searching for 'Geoffrey Chaucer', or even the father of poetry, in this way, encounter an especial difficulty – namely, that no one was ever quite sure of what he wrote.

To begin with, Chaucer's work circulated in manuscript form. Single instances of poems believed to be his were collated in the early years after his death as commercial one-offs, usually for private buyers who inevitably might influence content. Later on, as with all medieval writings, manuscript collections were printed in short runs or else compiled into folio editions, which were early versions of what we would recognise as a book. In each instance, some poems were omitted, whether by accident or design, and others included as if they were Chaucer's. The songs and 'lecherous lays' Chaucer mentions in the 'Retraction' to *The Canterbury Tales* have all disappeared, either lost or intentionally left out for reasons unknown. A Chaucer collection often, then, included anonymous work that we now know was written by others, especially his admirers like Lydgate, Gower or Hoccleve.

The first printed edition of Chaucer's work is William Caxton's version of *The Canterbury Tales*, published in 1478. In the 'Proheme' or preface to this edition, Caxton displays some anxiety about what he ought to include. He tells how someone brought him a seemingly better text closer to Chaucer's 'lost' original. Though Caxton accepts that an original manuscript is to be prized, he is also realistic enough to know that writers are frequently abridged or extended according to the whim of an editor (or buyer). The edition of Chaucer he prints in 1478 is, then, a 'best fit' and not necessarily a replica of Chaucer's *Tales*. Nevertheless, both Wynkyn de Worde (1498) and Richard Pynson (1492 and 1526) follow up with editions modelled on Caxton's version of Chaucer.

Right up until the late eighteenth century, the Chaucer we glean from the afterlives and adaptations of his work is based upon an apocryphal canon that comprises a staggering total of fifty-one spurious pieces. Shakespeare has just six works falsely ascribed to him. Many of these apocryphal works are courtly love and pastoral poems like the 'Assembly of Ladies', 'Court of Love', 'Craft of Lovers', 'Flower of Courtesy', 'Flower and the Leaf' and 'The Cuckoo and the Nightingale' which first appeared in a 1532 edition (Thynne) and remained part of Chaucer's canon for over 350 years. Such works shape Chaucer as a nature poet or a love poet in the style of the French *balades*. Yet this apocryphal canon was no more stable than Chaucer's 'real' one or consistent with it.

While a poem like 'The Cuckoo and the Nightingale' had a huge impact on constructions of Chaucer as both poet and man, so too did the many spurious continuations to *The Canterbury Tales*. Additional stories were written for the Pardoner, the Merchant and the Cook, a Robin Hood-style folk legend called

'The Tale of Gamelyn'. One poem, *The Testament of Cresseid*, profoundly altered readings of *Troilus and Criseyde* by appearing to be Book VI of Chaucer's major work. It was, in fact, a work in its own right, written by the Scottish medieval poet Robert Henryson in response to Chaucer's 'original'. Many editions include, too, 'The Plowman's Tale' which apparently provides a story for the figure Chaucer mentions in the 'General Prologue' but who does not tell a tale. Yet it is, in fact, a scathing, anti-religious work like the notorious 'Jack Upland' poem of the apocrypha, which exposes the corruption of friars and is often cited as evidence of Chaucer's Lollard sympathies.

Chaucer was continuously in print in the time of the Tudors, mainly thanks to the efforts of the folio editors. In 1532 William Thynne produced *The Workes of Geffray Chaucer newly printed with dyuers workes whiche were neuer in print before*. He followed this with at least one other edition published in 1542 and possibly again in 1550. A short time later in 1561, John Stow's collected Chaucer works appeared. Thomas Speght published a series of editions of *The Workes of Our Ancient and Learned English Poet, Geffrey Chaucer* in 1598, 1602 and 1687, and John Urry's folio of Chaucer appeared in 1721. Though every single edition of the folios mingled love poetry and pastoral idylls in the main, each also favours a slightly different Chaucer and builds a canon of his works complete with an ever-increasing number of spurious pieces. Chaucer's deliberate choice of the vernacular for his work contributed to a sense of Englishness witnessed in the political manoeuvrings of the Lancastrians, while the scurrilous – and spurious – anti-papist poems like 'Jack Upland' and 'The Ploughman's Tale' allowed Chaucer to be read as an active, proto-Protestant reformer. In turn, religious satires affirmed the centrality of royal power at the expense of the Church. Chaucer is, then, variously portrayed as a nature poet, a moralist, a satirical and anti-ecclesiastical writer, and a man of the court.

These early collations of Chaucer's work move ever further from what we might think of as Chaucer's originals – and, in many respects, from Chaucer the man. His is a literary legacy that is collated piecemeal and according to the political and personal inclinations of the compiler. The Chaucer of the manuscript tradition existed in that mode of transmission for less than a hundred years but it influenced, in turn, the Chaucer of the printed editions and folios and a host of others. Readers and writers like Shakespeare, Spencer, Milton, Dryden and Pope all received a 'Chaucer' who was defined by this folio canon and its apocrypha. The identity of Chaucer – both man and artist – was 'based on works he did not write', in the words of Kathleen Forni. So, too, this identity has always shifted according to the cultural contexts in which it appears. Until around 1700, for instance, references to *Troilus and Criseyde* were double those of the *Tales*, which are largely the focus of contemporary interest in Chaucer. Inevitably the Chaucer read through *Troilus* is different from the Chaucer whose biography we construct today.

One of the first 'biographies' of Chaucer is constructed by Thomas Speght. He wrongly attributes Thomas Usk's *Testament of Love* to Chaucer in the 1532 edition and then uses the 'facts' in this poem as a basis for Chaucer's life. He claims that Chaucer was a student at Oxford where he became a follower of John Wyclif, and, later, participated in a popular revolt against Richard II – presumably the Peasants' Revolt of 1381 – for which he was subsequently imprisoned. Chaucer was pardoned only when he testified against other rebels. Speght infers all this from a diatribe in the *Testament of Love* against the folly of following the herd and the fickleness of the mob, a view seemingly affirmed in lines from Chaucer's 'Man of Law's Tale' and 'The Clerk's Tale' in *The Canterbury Tales*. The story is repeated in Chaucer biographies until 1845 when someone finally points out that documentary evidence shows Chaucer collecting – in person – his pension at the precise time he is supposedly in gaol.

The notion of Geoffrey Chaucer as a rebel stays on record for hundreds of years. When John Leland writes Chaucer's first *official* biography he records that some of Chaucer's work was subjected to censorship by the authorities. Leland claims that 'The Ploughman's Tale' was denounced for its emphasis on clerical immorality and subsequently detached from *The Canterbury Tales*. Chaucer's 'Retraction' at the end of the *Tales* was seen as part of this conspiracy of suppression, while others believed it to be a forgery. Caxton (1477 and 1483) printed it as an integral part of the poem, as did Wynkyn de Worde (1498) and Pynson (1492) before omitting it in 1526. Though over fifty other poems are claimed as Chaucer's in the first three hundred years after his death, the 'Retraction' does not appear in the folios until Urry's edition in 1721.

A few years earlier, Thomas Hearne (1709) stated that the 'Retraction' was a forgery written by monks in response to the 'offence' of 'The Ploughman's Tale', a myth that circulates until the end of the nineteenth century and the excision of Chaucer's apocryphal canon. John Urry agrees. He adds a note to 'The Ploughman's Tale' to the effect that he thinks the 'Retraction' was probably written by the 'Scriveners' in retaliation for 'The Ploughman's Tale' because it appears in none of the manuscripts nor in most of the folio editions. There is no doubt that the 'Retraction' is an uneasy conclusion to the *Tales*, if indeed it is meant to be read as an end-point at all. It is actually missing from the famous Hengwrt manuscript which vies with the copy of the *Tales* in Ellesmere as the basis of modern editions. The leaves may simply have been lost or else its omission is, for some reason, deliberate.

Did the folio editors leave out the 'Retraction' – despite its inclusion in collections elsewhere – in order to present Chaucer as a fierce critic of the Church? Certainly, its moral, contemplative tone and Chaucer's seemingly apologetic renouncement of all but the most serious of his writings is profoundly at odds with depictions of the man as an early reformer of the Church. The famous sixteenth-century martyr John Foxe was one of those who continued to indict Chaucer as a Wycliffite regardless of the lack of evidence to that effect. In the 1570 revised edition of his *Actes and Monumentes* (1563) which was republished well into the seventeenth century, Foxe remarks Chaucer as one of the first 'faithful witnesses'. Such claims were repeated, albeit less vehemently, through the centuries.

Done to Death
c. 1400

The British Library in London holds a medieval manuscript that goes by the unprepossessing title of 'BL. MS. Additional. 5141'. In it is a full-length picture of Chaucer seemingly cut out from a larger portrait in another manuscript. The BL. MS. Add. 5141 was donated to the library in 1786 by one George Steevens. With it was a second document, a manuscript copy of *The Canterbury Tales* known as BL. MS. Add. 5140. The picture of Chaucer in the 5141 manuscript is the same one that Penguin used to grace the cover of Nevill Coghill's famous modernisation of Chaucer's *Tales* (1951) – except that the top corners have been clipped to make the image fit the book. Closer inspection of the actual picture in Steevens' manuscript reveals that three things are missing in the Penguin cover version. One is a representation of the Chaucer family's coat of arms. Another is a painting of an English daisy (marguerite), something that Chaucer's dream-vision narrators often worship. The third is a number written in Arabic numerals about which I shall have more to say later. On the back of the manuscript is a short biography of Chaucer which, judging by the handwriting style, was written somewhere in the late sixteenth century.

The errors in this mini-life seem ludicrous to modern audiences. One claim is that after the 1381 rebellion when protestors stormed London's city gates, Chaucer was exiled to the Low Countries with Richard's army in hot pursuit. Eventually he found refuge in France while the Crown confiscated what was said to be Chaucer's estate – which in fact belonged to his son Thomas. The biography concludes with a list of Chaucer's works. It includes poems it says are lost – apocrypha like 'Jack Upland', *The Book of the Lion* mentioned in the 'Retraction' and never seen, and, strangely, *The Book of the Duchess*. Chaucer's year of death is recorded as 1402, the same as the inscription on the picture. Modern scholarship has tended to dismiss this unknown Renaissance biographer and his mistakes. Yet he had, in fact, done his homework. His information came from several competing accounts of Chaucer's life story: Chaucer's early folio editors William Thynne and Thomas Speght, John Leland who was Henry VIII's chief librarian and archivist, and John Bale, author of an English literary history. Taken together these all point to a 600-year mystery over the precise details of Chaucer's death.

Speght's 1598 edition of Chaucer's *Workes* states that Geoffrey Chaucer died on 25th October 1400, which is the date commonly accepted today. An inscription on Chaucer's tomb in Westminster Abbey also has this date, but there is one problem: this is not actually Chaucer's tomb at all but a memorial erected by a Nicholas Brigham in 1556. Chaucer's publisher William Caxton was the first to note the lack of a suitable resting place for his poet, one that might befit a reputed 'maker' and high-profile courtier. Chaucer's friend the writer John Gower has an elaborate tomb in what is now Southwark Cathedral. So, Caxton commissioned an Italian poet called Stefano de Surigone (Surigo) to draft a short eulogy and attach it to a column in Westminster Abbey. Later, Chaucer's editor Stow and his friend Henry Scogan both claim that Chaucer is buried in the Abbey cloister. More specifically, according to an eighteenth-century historian named John Dart, his body lies beneath one of the slabs on the floor of the Abbey's south transept, presumably the tiny grave mentioned by Surigo a few years before.

Right from the start, the time, place and even the manner of Chaucer's death has been the subject of speculation and hearsay. John Bale offers several dates: 1450, 4th June 1400 – though it is on record that Chaucer received the arrears on the February instalment of his annuity a day later – and 1402, the date he finally settles on. 1402 is also the date Thomas Hoccleve gives in his 'Letter of Cupid', a poem always attributed to Chaucer until Skeat, Chaucer's most influential modern editor, excised it from the canon several hundred years later. John Foxe, in his *Actes and Monuments of Martyrs*, insists there is no definitive date of death for either Chaucer or Gower. Once again Geoffrey Chaucer seemingly slips out of sight.

It is difficult to believe that this meticulous civil servant and well-connected royal ambassador died without a single mention in any documents or chronicles of his time. This astute politician and clever administrator appointed attorneys to oversee his affairs while he was out of the country on King's business in, for example, 1378. Did he really die intestate? Every extant reference to Chaucer's death comes well after the event. No one mentions a funeral, though his son Thomas was acquiring a reputation of his own at this point and the Chaucers had a family connection to the new King Henry IV through Katherine Swynford, Chaucer's sister-in-law, and John of Gaunt. There is no will nor any list of his estate. Of course, any one of these documents might have been lost in the passage of time. Yet the survival rate of records associated with medieval London and its environs is unusually high. Chaucer's name fails to appear in every one of the registers in which we might expect to find it. He makes no bequests to churches or hospitals as was common, and none to any of his family or friends. Close friends like John Gower and Sir Lewis Clifford made their wills in keeping with the trend. Chaucer undoubtedly had something to leave: his manuscripts (all missing), a library perhaps. The God of Love mentions in *The Legend of Good Women* that Chaucer has sixty books or more. Is this pure fiction or a joke, a writer without any books? Or is it a clue of some sort?

Just prior to his death, Chaucer took out a fifty-three-year lease on a house in the garden of the Lady Chapel in Westminster Abbey. He was clearly not expecting to die any time soon. Chaucer was fifty-nine or sixty years of age. Though the average life expectancy in the Middle Ages was around thirty, this was an era of wars, violent disputes, Black Death and high infant mortality. But the rule of thumb seemed to be that those who reached their forties were likely to make old bones. Whatever happened to Chaucer took him by surprise as there is no evidence of illness. He was alive and well in the opening months of 1400 when, according to the *Life-Records*, he probably took a trip to Calais, business unknown. There is no record of plague for that year, although after the devastation of 1349 there were recurrent outbreaks of Black Death in which adolescents and the elderly were especially vulnerable. Was there an accident, perhaps, or, as some suspect, murder or an arranged disappearance?

Both Thomas Hoccleve and John Lydgate were key players in securing Chaucer's literary reputation in the years immediately after his death. Lydgate was a monk of Bury St Edmunds. As such, he would have been aware of the Archbishop of Canterbury Thomas Arundel's vigorous crackdown on heresy that began in the monastic libraries. Lydgate consistently refers to the 'tragedy' of Chaucer's death in both his *The Siege of Thebes* and *The Troy Book*. Hoccleve's vocabulary in *The Regement of Princes* is equally interesting. The eulogy in the *Regement* speaks of 'slaughter', 'slay', a life that was 'queynt', quenched or snuffed out. In his address to Chaucer, Hoccleve writes of how Death was too hasty 'To renne on [run at] thee, and reue [rob] the thi lyf'. Terry Jones remarks that these lines read as if Chaucer was mugged or attacked in a dark alleyway. They certainly correspond to the hyperbolic terms in which both Hoccleve and Lydgate write of Chaucer's death. Both though pursued the same Lancastrian agenda to prosecute the claim to power of Henry's son, the Prince of Wales – later Henry V.

Chaucer's name was integral to this enterprise and, so, the 'tragedy' of his 'slaughter' may simply be a literary technique. Equally it might recall a commonplace of their culture, the 'fact' that Chaucer's demise was in some way unexpected, even inexplicable. One possibility lies in the tumultuous years of Henry IV's reign.

Epiphanies and Uprisings
1399–1411

A winter's evening, 17th December 1399. At the home of William Colchester, abbot of Westminster Abbey, a dinner party is in full swing. Among the guests are the earls of Rutland, Huntingdon, Kent and Salisbury. Sir Thomas Despenser, Duke of Gloucester, and a number of barons are also present: Thomas Blount, Benedict Sely and Ralph Lumley. There is something more than dinner on the menu tonight. These men are plotting sedition. Others join them: Thomas Merks, the former bishop of Carlisle, and two priests favoured by Richard II, Richard Maudelyn and William Ferriby. Roger Walden is there, the ex-archbishop of Canterbury ousted when Thomas Arundel reclaimed the post on his return from exile, and one 'Master Pol'. Here the records refer to a 'Jean Paule', the French physician in whose care Richard placed his young queen Isabella when he was arrested. To a man, all were loyal to the deposed King who was languishing in prison at Pontecraft Castle. Richard and their hopes were still alive. The earls had been chamber knights close to the King. Some of them had been taken into custody during Henry's bid for the crown. Rutland, Huntingdon and John Montagu, poet and Earl of Salisbury, had just been released. Henry and Arundel might have guessed where they were headed. They did not disappoint.

By January 1400 Henry had uncovered their plot to assassinate him, probably thanks to the Earl of Rutland, who may have betrayed the rebels. Henry waited for them to take flight across the towns and cities of England and then sat back while they were lynched in the mob rule his close advisor Arundel was actively encouraging. Some, like Maudelyn and Ferriby, were executed, drawn by a horse through the streets, quartered and hanged in the spectacularly violent fashion that became a hallmark of Henry's reign. It is said that Thomas Blount begged for death as he watched his bowels burn on the fire before him. The heads of the traitors were displayed on the railings on London Bridge. The few surviving rebels – Merks was imprisoned in the Tower of London – were forever indebted to Arundel. Their example ensured the rest of the clergy soon fell into line with his anti-heretical stance. This aborted 'Epiphany Uprising' marked the end for Richard II who died in mysterious circumstances, without a funeral and with his body exhibited on a nationwide tour. Henry IV buried him out of sight on a private estate in King's Langley, far from Richard's special place, Westminster Abbey, and far from his beloved queen, Anne of Bohemia, with whom he had planned to be interred. Rumours that he was still alive swept the country. Anyone caught spreading them was punished, like the twenty Scottish friars Arundel had executed in 1402.

Chaucer was still writing *The Canterbury Tales* and possibly collating the Ellesmere or Hengwrt manuscript copies at the time of his death. He was also living in a house in the grounds of Westminster Abbey, just next door to the place the would-be assassins used to rendezvous. Two months after Henry IV was crowned, Chaucer had taken a long lease on a house in the Lady Garden of the Abbey. Once again, just as when he was living at Aldgate during the Peasants' Revolt of 1381, he was literally right next door to a rebellion. It is extraordinarily difficult to believe that Chaucer had no inkling of the Epiphany plot. This is the same man who spied for Richard II and his grandfather, the same savvy politician who resigned his controllerships after the Merciless Parliament of 1388 and slipped quietly out of London while many of his social circle were executed. His move into the Abbey grounds was more than timely.

Westminster Abbey had a long and close association with Richard II. He actively supported the Westminster monks, for instance, and recognised the Abbey's right to autonomy. Its lands were independent of both state and royal jurisdiction, which made it a place of sanctuary for many. Sir Robert Tresilian, Chief Justice of the King's Bench, fled there in the 1380s when Richard lost power to the Lords Appellant. Thomas Arundel, then Archbishop of York, had Tresilian dragged out and executed, ignoring Richard's plea to spare him on the grounds that the Abbey was exempt from ecclesiastical law. Despite this isolated incident, Westminster continued as an approved 'chartered' sanctuary which made it, theoretically at least, a permanent place of refuge. The so-called Sanctuary men often traded from there or continued their criminal activities. Chaucer's house was not directly in this part of the Abbey, but the principle of safety still applied if he needed it.

Of course, Chaucer's house move may be another of those coincidences that appear on a regular basis in his life records. There is nothing to prove directly that Chaucer moved into the Abbey gardens because he needed a refuge, but even if this was not the reason, he was certainly flagging his allegiance to the old regime of the Ricardian court. Circumstantial evidence strongly suggests that sanctuary was a useful option. Many argue that the house was merely a grace-and-favour residence offered to elderly or retired courtiers. Chaucer had not retired, for he travelled to Calais during the final months of his life, on business – presumably the King's – unknown. The list of subsequent tenants also rather disproves the case. The next man to lease the same house is Paul de la Mounte, Henry IV's doctor. Yet recent inquiry suggests that this man was in fact Richard's physician and the same 'Jean-Paul' or 'Master Pol' who was present at the rebel dinner in the closing weeks of 1399 and a likely candidate for sanctuary indeed. William Horscroft is next in the records, a wealthy trader in skins and former supplier to the deposed King whom he had also financially aided. The other tenant is perhaps a surprising one. His name was Thomas Chaucer.

It seems that Thomas had inherited his father's diplomatic skills. He was an aspiring and successful courtier who began his career in the household of John of Gaunt, the new King's father. But like Chaucer, Thomas was a man who sailed close to the wind. At first, Henry approved of him. He appointed Thomas as Chief Butler to the King in 1402, a post in which he served on and off throughout Henry's reign, and again for Henry V in 1413. Three days after his coronation, Henry IV also gave Thomas a life appointment as Constable of Wallingford Castle. By 1407, and again in 1410, he was Speaker of the Commons. In between that time, he clashed with Thomas Arundel, hence, perhaps, the sanctuary residence.

Arundel made himself Chancellor of the Realm in 1408. As Speaker, Thomas Chaucer argued in the Commons that the King's Council that Arundel presided over ought to be subject to parliamentary scrutiny. The records reveal that Thomas was cut off in mid-speech. He lost his position a short time later. In 1410 he was re-elected as Speaker but ran into controversy once more. He spearheaded a bill to 'disendow' the Church by confiscating its property and re-distributing the wealth amongst the King and the laity – something originally proposed by John Wyclif. Henry IV banned all discussion of this idea. Thomas was forced to make a humiliating public apology on behalf of the Commons. He almost certainly avoided execution because of his family connection to the King. John of Gaunt, Henry's father, was Thomas' uncle through his marriage to Katherine Swynford. Henry's half-siblings, the powerful Beauforts – Katherine and Gaunt's illegitimate children – were Thomas' cousins. It is no surprise, then, that by the autumn of 1411 Thomas was safely tucked up in Geoffrey Chaucer's former house.

Rats and Retractions

One of the earliest manuscript copies of Chaucer's *The Canterbury Tales* is the famous Hengwrt Manuscript. It survives in the form of an early book: that is with its leaves collated, probably over a period of several years, and then bound together. Close inspection of this manuscript, which is currently held in the Huntingdon Library, California, reveals signs of lengthy neglect. Rats have gnawed the vellum and damaged it in a number of places, which suggests that the document had been untouched by human hand for many years. There are further indications that Hengwrt was started and then put aside. Someone has copied out 'The Monk's Tale' with one particular stanza missing. That verse has been added in the margin while the *Tales* was still in loose-leaf form. The cramped handwriting matches that of the scribe who worked on the presentation copy of Thomas Hoccleve's *Regement of Princes*, written in 1412–13, long after Chaucer's work. Were the two pieces copied at the same time? If, as the evidence suggests, they were, then the Hengwrt manuscript must have been left unbound for more than a decade of Henry IV's rule. Wherever it was placed, it was vulnerable to attack by rodents. According to Terry Jones, the conclusion is inevitable: Hengwrt was hidden away out of sight for over ten years. It reappears at the precise moment that Henry's son the Prince of Wales petitions for power and, so, marks Chaucer as an important aspect of that political manoeuvre.

The Hengwrt manuscript is interesting for a number of other reasons. Many medieval writers left a manuscript legacy of their works. William Langland the *Piers Plowman* poet did, and so too did Boccaccio and Machaut. John Gower also participated in this developing trend, leaving work complete with corrections in his own hand. We have nothing of Chaucer's poems in his own handwriting, nor, even, in anyone else's. In fact, save for the prose works *Boece* and *A Treatise on the Astrolabe*, Chaucer leaves not a single manuscript from his own lifetime. Anything that survives today has come from copies made after Chaucer's death right at the start of the fifteenth century. If we accept that Chaucer was reputed during his life and that his works were circulated by someone, if not him, then the question is: what happened to his manuscripts?

There is some evidence to indicate that the two earliest versions of *The Canterbury Tales* – that is, the aforementioned Hengrwt and the well-known illustrated Ellesmere Manuscript, which is the basis of most modern editions – *do* stem from Chaucer's last years; in which case, what happened to all the other poems and the various copies and versions of his indi-vidual works? Possibly the incomplete *Tales* was transmitted only as a loosely bound or flimsy booklet to which more could be added as work progressed, and which, hence, did not survive the wear and tear of circulation. This does not account for other works, however. Scholars agree that no authorial copy text of *The Canterbury Tales* exists which is why the stories are dis-ordered and lack a definite overarching frame. Other medieval writers compiled their collected works while they were still alive. Despite the anxiety he expresses over the reception of his writing, Chaucer fails to leave behind a single key copy of any of his poems for posterity.

One answer is that he died before he had a chance to order his affairs. He certainly seems to have been interrupted while working on his life-long project the *Tales*. Both Hengwrt and the Ellesmere have a break in their copying, and at exactly the same point. Whoever was overseeing production stopped, leaving the first of these manuscripts – probably Hengwrt – unsupervised and possibly without direction. Was this person Geoffrey Chaucer? Scribes have copied 'The Cook's Tale' only to halt at line fifty-eight. They have left a space as if expecting more copy to arrive. None ever did. Scribes were unlikely to begin the laborious and costly business of copying without the completed text. This means that it is highly unlikely that Chaucer was still writing 'The Cook's Tale' as they worked. Something else, something more dramatic must have occurred to interrupt the proceedings.

Estelle Stubbs, editor of *The Hengwrt Chaucer Digital Facsimile* (CD-ROM), points out that the production of both Hengwrt and Ellesemere was severely affected by an unknown event. At some point, the artists who began work on the Ellesmere illustrations were replaced. Stubbs agrees that the Hengwrt Manuscript shows that whoever supervised the copying stopped – and suddenly. The final pages are copied in haste for several scribes seem to be working at once. Different inks have been used and there seems to be some confusion over the shape of the manuscript. Two tales were undoubtedly copied for another collection and added to Hengwrt at the last minute, probably in an effort to make it look as if it was finished. The note in the margin of 'The Cook's Tale' makes this clear. It reads 'Of this Cokes tale maked Chaucer namoore'. Again, the ink is different from the rest of the manuscript, indicating that it was a late addition and, therefore, unlikely to have been Chaucer. To begin with, both Hengwrt and Ellesmere have obviously been compiled from 'best texts and under authorial supervision'. Towards the end of their production they have been 'cobbled together piecemeal'. Terry Jones is convincing when he says this strongly suggests that at the time of Chaucer's death, or just after, Chaucer's own manuscript copies were no longer available. No doubt this is the moment too that Chaucer disappears from the records, presumed dead.

Cultural historians like Terry Jones believe that the Ellesmere manuscript is a clue to Chaucer's fate. Ellesmere is famed for its decoration. Miniatures of the Canterbury pilgrims accompany the tale each one recounts. These portraits match Chaucer's descriptions of these individuals in the 'General Prologue' – all, that is, except three: the illustrations of the Monk, the Friar and the Knight. Chaucer's Monk, an expensively dressed gad-about-town, is dressed completely in black in Ellesmere and apparently shrouded by a veil. The picture of the worldly Friar is similarly blackened while his harp, or zither, has been replaced by a staff. Scrutiny with a microscope reveals that someone has altered the Ellesmere manuscript. Beneath the Ellesmere Knight is a drawing of a figure much closer to the one depicted in Chaucer's poem. The Monk and the Friar are also superimposed images. The originals have been partially obscured by layers of black pigment. The Monk's veil is actually an attempt to paint out the bald head which is a hallmark of Chaucer's description of him. The owner of the Ellesmere must have had a pressing reason to spoil such an elegant and valuable manuscript. The changes made to the illustrations of the Monk and the Friar certainly suggest that the most compelling reason for the alterations was fear.

By 1407, the estimated date of the Ellesmere censor's work, the corrupt and venial figures populating Chaucer's fictional clergy in the *Tales* would have incited accusations of heresy. Families like the De Veres – who owned the Ellesmere script – were rethinking old allegiances as Thomas Arundel, self-styled Archbishop of Canterbury, Chancellor of the Realm, and Henry's deputy, tightened his grip on power. Arundel vigorously prosecuted charges of heresy or treason and outlawed ridicule or criticism of the Church. Just two years later, in 1409, he published the *Constitutions*, which banned, amongst other things, any book or tract written by Wyclif, English translations of the Bible, and any anti-ecclesiastical comment or notion. The owners of the Ellesmere Manuscript had every reason to be anxious. But what has this to do with Chaucer and how is it connected to the strange disappearance of his manuscripts?

Lollards in the Wind
1374–99

'I smelle a Lollere in the wynd.'

CT, II, 1173

When John Lydgate proclaims, in his *Troy Book*, that Chaucer was the first poet to 'magnifie / And adourne' the English language, his words do far more than simply enhance a fellow poet's literary reputation. Lydgate directs readers to Chaucer's *Troilus and Criseyde* as an example of vernacular writing so fine that it ought to be available in every borough, town, village or city for all to read. He includes monks and other cloistered members of the Church in this appeal and it is here that his real purpose becomes apparent. Lydgate made these claims for Chaucer at a time when Thomas Arundel was ransacking libraries and calling in certain books for examination and revision.

'Was Chaucer a Lollard?' is a redundant question according to Terry Jones; in the 1390s, the most important thing was that a person *might be called one*. There was no unified sect called the Lollards in late medieval culture. Rather, the term was applied to supporters of John Wyclif or anyone advocating any aspect of religious reform. Wyclif was an Oxford graduate, a clever theologian whom Edward III sent to negotiate with the Pope in 1374 before rewarding him with a salaried living at Lutterworth in Leicestershire. Wyclif argued that the transubstantiation of the Host was symbolic and not literal as the Church proclaimed. He further attacked clerical privilege when he called upon the Church to hand over its wealth and follow Christ's example of poverty. He said that the Bible was authorised only by God. Bibles and their accompanying glosses or explanations should therefore be in English for all to follow.

The use of the vernacular was central to Wyclif's ideas for reform. At first the Church openly debated these issues. The nobility, too, supported any move to redistribute Church estates from which they stood to benefit. In 1377, when Wyclif was summoned on a charge of heresy by the Bishop of London, John of Gaunt accompanied him with an armed guard. A similar attempt the following year had to be aborted when Sir Lewis Clifford was sent to prohibit any formal sentencing of Wyclif. Increasingly, though, the Church tightened its grip. Thomas Arundel's failed petition to Parliament in 1395 was only his first attempt to ban biblical translation. The Eucharist quickly became a litmus test of orthodox faith. Those who denied that its transformation was anything other than literal were denounced as Lollards or Wycliffites.

As the fourteenth century drew to a close, anti-ecclesiastical comment was vigorously pursued. In the autumn of 1399 the heads of all abbeys and major churches were instructed to submit their chronicles for examination. Henry Bolingbroke was searching for something to support his claim to the crown and testing loyalties. Of the six chronicles extant from Richard's time, only one is not entirely supportive of the new King, as Terry Jones has reported. Arundel was similarly punishing any writing that he perceived as heretical. Where formerly writers had enjoyed the freedom of engagement in a long tradition of satire, those same works might now be viewed as radical.

In the midst of this climate of fear Geoffrey Chaucer was working on *The Canterbury Tales*. He knew Arundel personally, having twice witnessed proceedings for the transfer of property that Arundel owned. But personal connection may not have been enough to save him from accusations of blasphemy. Terry

Jones is persuasive when he suggests that the *Tales* was potentially Chaucer's death warrant. Here Chaucer challenges every notion of authority – literary, social, political, and certainly religious. Many of his stories engage contemporary debates about Church corruption, while his pilgrim portraits often match the denunciations of Wycliffite polemic.

His Friar enjoys singing and harping, fine wine, good food and sex, while his preaching exposes the hypocrisy of those corrupt mendicants who were supposed to live in abject poverty according to the example of Christ. Chaucer's Pardoner is another anticlerical portrait. The Pardoner is unlicensed despite claiming authority from his fake papal bulls and relics. As such, he is forbidden to sell pardons or forgive sins, and certainly had no right to claim he could deliver the last sacrament if one of the pilgrims died en route to Canterbury. His letters of authority allegedly come from his diocesan bishop. In the 1390s this would be Thomas Arundel himself, a dangerous connection indeed for anyone to make, albeit in fiction.

The Pardoner's friend, the Summoner, another favourite target of the reformers, enforces Church law by bringing those charged to the ecclesiastical courts. The Summoner relates an anecdote about a friar who is taken on a tour of hell by an angel. He supposes there are no friars there because they are all in heaven. The angel takes him to Satan who will show him where friars congregate. Satan lifts up his tail and bares his behind; twenty thousand friars swarm in and out of his anus like bees in a hive. Unusually for Chaucer, there is no known source for this story save perhaps the late medieval tale of a Cistercian monk who finds his fellow brethren nestling under the cloak of the Virgin Mary. Similarly, no analogues exist for the remainder of 'The Summoner's Tale', including the ending where the gift of the fart – fitting reward for the hot air of the Friar's preaching – is divided on the hollow spokes of a cartwheel. This parodies the Pentecost when Jesus' disciples receive the Holy Spirit as a great wind and, with it, the power to understand many different languages. For orthodox

Catholics this demonstrates how God speaks through the chosen. For Wyclif, it showed how God communicates with everyone, hence his demand for vernacular Bibles.

'The Summoner's Tale' alone sees Chaucer guilty of two charges: blasphemy and writing in English. Even 'The Parson's Tale' may have been more provocative at the turn of the fourteenth century than we might imagine from a distance of more than 600 years. Other pilgrims clearly identify the Parson as a reformer. Harry Bailly says he smells a Lollard in the wind but still invites him to preach. The Shipman demurs: let's not, he says, in case he sows cockle-weed in our clean corn and so contaminates the 'true' word of God. The Parson quotes the gospels; Arundel made knowledge of the Bible a heresy. His brother is the Plowman, that hero of Langland's *Piers Plowman*, often thought to embody social and spiritual excellence. Yet, at the same time, Chaucer allows this humble, unlearned figure to stand as a touchstone of exemplary behaviour in contrast to the Friar and others. The Parson offers the most orthodox meditation in support of confession: that it should be heard by a priest. Read in conjunction with the 'Retraction', 'The Parson's Tale' perhaps attempts to duck out of *open* challenge and move towards reconciliation with the new regime.

Whatever critical preferences we bring to bear on the *Tales*, there is no doubt that throughout his life Chaucer's actions put him firmly in the Ricardian camp. This alone may have been enough to indict him in the eyes of Henry IV and Arundel. History has often viewed Richard II as an orthodox king. The Latin epitaph on his tomb in Westminster Abbey certainly says so, telling the world that he was one who 'crushed heretics'. We know that the Abbey tomb only exists because Henry V interred his remains and placed them there. We know too that despite what that epitaph says Richard was, in private, personally close to a number of well-known reformists: William Neville, Lewis Clifford, Richard Stury, John Clanvowe, John Montagu and Thomas Latimer. So, too, was Geoffrey Chaucer.

Retraction
1398–1407

We do not know when Chaucer wrote the 'Retraction', or why. Most academics have assumed that Chaucer penned it as a conventional literary device, a means of ending a work just as an apology – usually for the inadequate techniques of its narrator – might preface it. This explanation makes sense if the 'Retraction' was an early poem, or if *The Canterbury Tales* was complete. It is far less convincing if Chaucer wrote it in the closing years of the century when Archbishops Courteney and then Arundel began to close down religious dissent.

The 'Retraction' is a puzzle. Its denial of almost all of Chaucer's work makes little sense, either as a finale to the rich and complex array of stories that precedes it or as a literary trick. On the one hand, it is the work of a man making peace with himself and the world before he dies. Yet in it Chaucer recants almost everything, even *The House of Fame* and *The Book of the Duchess*, poems that can hardly be regarded as sinful. In the end, he claims only his translation of Boethius, the rest dismissed as 'lecherous lays' and 'worldly vanities'. The choice of 'Retractions' as a title is also interesting. The word 'retraccioun' is found nowhere else in Middle English. It seems that Chaucer took it from the Latin 'retractatio' used by St Augustine to mean variously: revision, correction, to reconsider, or remembrance. Chaucer says, too, that he revokes his works, a term he employs on only one other occasion, in *Troilus and Criseyde*. When

Troilus faints, Criseyde kisses him 'Hym to revoken', meaning in order to *revive* him.

It appears, then, that the object of the 'Retraction' is less to apologise or withdraw authorship, and more about cataloguing works – as Chaucer does in other poems – and reviewing them. In this sense, everything that he recants is simultaneously denied and made to live on: those vaguely mentioned 'songs and lecherous lays', every poem right down to *The Book of the Lion*, a text lost to us, perhaps even a work in progress. A retraction written as late as 1398 or 1400 is entirely different from one written prior to the Appellant rebellion of 1387. A later poem memorialises Chaucer's works while appearing to deny them, a useful strategy given the context of repression. Public retraction was a popular means of bringing critics of the Church into line and suppressing dissent. Certainly after Richard's deposition in 1399, those who 'confessed' in this way avoided burning at the stake. And those who recanted included Chaucer's close friend Lewis Clifford.

Clifford was one of those men closest to Richard II. He was his chamber knight and one to Richard's grandfather Edward III before him. Throughout his life he had been open about his desire to see Church reform. Historians often refer to him as one of the 'Lollard Knights' of Chaucer's intimate circle. Yet in 1402, Lewis publicly renounced every pronouncement and private opinion on pain of death. Arundel made him list all of Wyclif's ideas and provide the names of everyone sympathetic to the Lollard cause. Lewis escaped with his life. Not so Chaucer and Clifford's old friend and fellow knight John Montagu, Earl of Salisbury. He had been torn to pieces by vigilantes for his part in the aborted coup against Henry IV in January 1400. Clifford's fate allows some insight into the political climate that prevailed in Chaucer's final years. According to Terry Jones, maybe this is what prompted the 'Retraction'. Maybe this is why Chaucer was desperate to compile his manuscripts before they were 'conveniently' lost or hidden away.

History was being rewritten elsewhere too. Chaucer's old friend John Gower had appeared increasingly hostile in the 1390s to the Ricardian court culture in which he had prospered. By the time Henry IV was crowned, and for years after, Gower was his biggest fan. Several versions of his *Confessio Amantis* survive. We have thirty-two copies of the first version alone, which he dedicated to Chaucer and King Richard. Yet in all subsequent versions these references have been erased. Other favourable comments about Richard have been scrubbed or altered in Henry's favour, many in Gower's own handwriting. Gower cleverly altered the chronology of his publications and actively revised his *Vox Clamantis* too. English chronicle writers similarly excised pro-Richard material and rewrote anything criticising John of Gaunt, Henry's father, or any of his family. Pages were cut out. Monks revisited their libraries and histories to comply with Arundel's proscriptions. Somewhere along the way Richard's library was partially destroyed. Records show that he received many gifts of books. Jean Froissart, for instance, presented him with a book of love poems in 1395, only four years before he was deposed. It cannot be found. When Richard wrested power back from the Lords Appellant, he was given a commemorative book about the pageant that marked his return in 1392. It has not survived.

Medieval manuscripts were extremely expensive to make. They would not be casually discarded or deliberately neglected. In this light, the actions of those writers, librarians and book collectors from 1399 onwards point to a wholesale repression of literary culture. Richard's books vanish without trace. In the famous illustration of Chaucer reading *Troilus and Criseyde* to the court, Richard II's face has been rubbed out. Writers like Gower falsify their literary history. Other writings connected with the Ricardian court disappear. Where are Sir John Monatagu's *balades* and poems? John Clanvowe, another of Richard's knights and friends with Chaucer, leaves only *The Boke of Cupid*, apparently, and then no manuscript of it from Richard's time. The only extant copies are from the fifteenth century, attached as part of Chaucer's apocrypha. Chaucer's lyrics and the other 'lost' works mentioned in the 'Retraction': all gone. Somewhere history was being rewritten and Geoffrey Chaucer, that canny public servant and royal spy, would surely have known it.

One of the last poems Chaucer wrote is 'The Complaint of Chaucer to his Purse'. The poem turns on a playful literary conceit in which Chaucer's purse becomes a lady whom he addresses with a series of sexual puns: 'light' (fickle), 'heavy' (pregnant), 'die' (orgasm). Each verse ends on the same teasing note with the refrain, 'Beth hevy ageyn, or elles, moote I dye.' Chaucer also attaches an Envoy after verse three where he speaks directly to the newly crowned Henry IV and requests payment of his yearly annuities, which had so far been confirmed but not actually paid out. Here Chaucer calls Henry the conqueror of Brutus' Albion (England) and King by right of birth (descent from Henry III) and 'free eleccion' after the realm had been mismanaged. At first glance Chaucer seems to be repeating the claims Henry makes in his proclamation to the country. This reading was mentioned in a footnote in Robert Bell's Victorian edition of Chaucer's works (1854) and subsequently repeated as a fact by Walter Skeat and a host of others. Yet there is no record of this proclamation in the archives. Henry IV never said that he had conquered England or that he was elected by the will of Parliament; he had been advised not to.

Why, then, did Chaucer include this reference? If this was an attempt to flatter his new monarch then Chaucer would surely have written more fulsomely than five lines in a style completely unlike anything he had ever used with Richard. Jones is convincing when he speculates that the piece was a coded affirmation of support for the deposed King and his supporters. Early on in the poem Chaucer describes his purse / lady as yellow as the sun and as his 'hertes stere' (heart's guide). Richard II's hair was blonde or reddish-blonde. One of his badges was a shining sun.

The other was embossed with the symbol of the white hart (heart). Read in the context of the final moments of Richard's reign, perhaps even as he is imprisoned and the plot to kill Henry is hatched next door to Chaucer's house, the line 'Beth hevy ageyn, or elles, moote I dye' is especially resonant.

Barely a few months after the poem was completed Chaucer was dead. Terry Jones concludes that Chaucer did not collect the Michaelmas instalment of his annuity because he was either under house arrest in the Abbey or in prison in Saltwood Castle, which was the fate of other suspected Lollards. His manuscripts were destroyed and his death hushed up. I can find no evidence of murder and so conclude that his death was simply out of the blue, an accident or an unexpected fatal illness like plague. I do, however, believe that Chaucer's works were confiscated and that he knew this was imminent – hence the 'Retraction' and rush to gather them up. Chaucer was clearly not yet ready to desert Richard II, and was mindful of the consequences of that decision. The rest is a mystery he has taken to the grave.

Our Geoffrey

The author of Geoffrey Chaucer Hath a Blog speaks to us in cod-French and a mock olde-worlde English that belies its clever aping of medieval syntax and diction. The site comes complete with Chaucer's response to contemporary news items, his agony-aunt page, 'Who Am I?' links, and letters that purport to reveal his gay relationship with John Gower. At the time of writing, the list of contributors includes Katherine Swynford and 'little' Lewis. Chaucer complains about money and a global recession blamed on the brief rule of the Lords Appellant, about Philippa's nagging and Richard's driving. He reveals how Richard is to deliver a paper entitled 'Bring 500 Cheshire Archers to a Department Meeting' at the famous international conference for medievalists held at the University of Western Michigan, home of 'Kalamazoo – the folk of Babel'. As ever, the Chaucer of this blog inhabits the uneasy divide between popular and academic cultures.

Chaucer's arrival in cyberspace seems a fitting tribute to the multi-layered creature that is Geoffrey Chaucer. Steve Ellis notes how Martin Starkie's voiceover for the permanent Centre Exhibition attached to the 'Canterbury Tales Experience' in – where else? – Canterbury, wonders why, when there are so many extant records of Chaucer's life, instead of the man there is just 'a vast puzzling silence'. There is perhaps a neat irony in Starkie's question, especially in the light of the 'popular' Chaucer Starkie and his collaborator Nevill Coghill – best known for his lively and still relevant modernisation of the *Tales* (1951) – established back in 1985. The Canterbury Tales Visitor Attraction and Gift Shop and the Chaucer Heritage Centre in Canterbury offer readings, events, exhibitions and an annual Chaucer festival as part of the commendable move to take Chaucer out of the academy and into popular culture. The yearly Canterbury Tales Pilgrimage, which has taken place every April since 1987, travels Chaucer's famous fictional Southwark to Canterbury route of *The Canterbury Tales*. The Centre Exhibition regularly screens *The Canterbury Tales – The Musical*, co-written and co-produced by Coghill and Starkie in 1968, while the Visitor Attraction presents a tableau of life-size figures from the *Tales* complete with special effects and a continuous loop narration of forty minutes' worth of an abridged and modernised *Tales*. Its final point reconstructs Thomas Becket's shrine; the real thing is just next door in Canterbury Cathedral. The entire experience commemorates, on the one hand, Chaucer and his 'associates' like William Caxton and William Morris, and on the other romps through an olde-worlde Middle Ages complete with jousting, dancing and juggling. Steve Ellis remarks that 'in this general "heritage" hullabaloo Chaucer… seems to have slipped out unnoticed'. No-one could blame him.

Other modern afterlives tell a similar story to perpetrate popular notions of, in Ellis' words, 'Chaucer's uncomplicated bawdy affability', the genial and, above all, humane fellow who deals in universals: the only-joking critic of a congenial, beer-swilling merrie-England that never existed and for which we still pine. Witness, too, a contemporary obsession with the *Tales* as somehow encapsulating the man and his time even as our reductive readings privilege only the humorous or the scatological: the famous joke of 'The Miller's Tale' – Nicholas' kiss-my-arse invitation, his farting into Absolon's face, the bare buttocks branded in revenge. BBC1 television's *Tales* (1969) – again co-authored by Coghill and Starkie – was a large pub-crawl, full of revelry and japes, fisticuffs and shouting, complete with all the *fabliaux* and set to a backdrop of chocolate-box English villages. Admittedly, it included, too, stories from the Clerk, Franklin, Canon's Yeoman and the Manciple, and it kicked off with 'The Knight's Tale', a highly unpopular choice according to public viewing figures, and something omitted completely from their *The Canterbury Tales – The Musical* show which opened a year earlier in London's West End. This extravaganza still plays around the globe, audiences clearly delighted with its spirit of laughter and drunken, sexual horseplay.

Modern fictionalisations of Chaucer continue to depend on all those Chaucers of centuries before, even as they add layers of their own to occlude the man still further and shape biographies like this one. Steve Ellis suggests that nostalgic visions of unity wipe out not only the many and inherent contradictions or ambivalences of Chaucer's work but those of his life, too. And, of course, they intersect with contemporary culture in ways that reveal something of our own social and political concerns. Despite those earlier epithets about his Englishness, it is William Shakespeare and not Chaucer who is the national icon enshrined in academic and school curricula, hailed as the founding father of 'Literature' and the English language, and a cultural magnet for every tourist or international visitor. Geoffrey Chaucer is increasingly absent from literary culture and from public view, dismissed thanks to the perceived inaccessibility of his language. He is without the commercial cachet of realist novelists like Austen, Dickens and Hardy, who all adapt with ease to television and film, and is caught up in a tangle of an anti-dead, white, male resistance. In the words of Steve Ellis, he is both 'everywhere and nowhere', the fact that he is missing 'as significant as his presence'. How did he get this way?

Chaucer's name appears in present-day academia more often than that of any other medieval writer. Within a tradition of medieval literature and scholarship Chaucer stands and is called upon to speak for its entire canon, though he is distinct from it in so many ways. He acquired this institutional status largely through the efforts of scholars like Frederick Furnivall, Walter Skeat and Thomas Tyrwhitt. By the late nineteenth century Chaucer's apocryphal canon had been rumbled. Thomas Tyrwhitt made probably the first genuine attempt to confront those false attributions. Tyrwhitt laid the foundations in his 'Account of the Works of Chaucer' and his five volumes of *The Canterbury Tales of Chaucer* (1775–8). Walter Skeat finally excised fifty-one texts on the basis of inaccurate or incomplete attribution, publishing *The Complete Works of Geoffrey Chaucer* in seven volumes in 1894–7. His critical selection fixed a canon of works as authentically Chaucer's. Those left out or rejected outright were compiled into an apocryphal Chaucer canon that exists alongside the 'real' one, greatly aiding academic study. But that same crucial enterprise further obscures Chaucer-the-man in a number of ways.

In *The Chaucer Canon* (1900), Skeat seems to suggest that his selections were made on the basis of Chaucer's name rather than anything intrinsically valuable within the text. Skeat worked out his definitive list by looking for parallels between Chaucer's life and his art, just as so many had done before him, and would do again in later years. At precisely the same time, those works that were not Chaucer's were expunged to take on a life and meaning entirely separate from those of Chaucer. The diverse contexts of their former inclusion and the kinds of Chaucer they constructed disappeared at a stroke. Future biographies would of necessity make a simple equation – man and poetry, nothing in between. In the same book Skeat dismisses the apocrypha as 'beneath discussion'. That aesthetic judgement has much to answer for.

The scholastic endeavours of Tyrwhitt, Skeat and Furnivall also impacted positively on our modern understanding of Chaucer. From them we inherited a stable body of writings by Chaucer as opposed to the Chaucerian canon of before. When Frederick Furnivall established the Chaucer Society in 1868 with the purpose of introducing a general readership to what was perceived as a neglected poet, he could hardly have dreamed the extent of the Society's influence. His intent was to gather up manuscript and archival material from scholars around the world in order to construct not only a reliable, academic canon of texts as a landmark for later critical readers, but also one accessible to popular culture. Along the way, he also attempted to produce a reputable biography of the poet he described in *Macmillan's Magazine* in 1871 as the second greatest English writer, 'The most genial and humourful healthy-souled man that England had ever seen.'

Academic study of Chaucer and his works is the staple of his afterlife. The Chaucer Society still exists, together with its scholarly journal *Studies in the Age of Chaucer*. The titles of other publications give a taste of the breadth of critical interest in a poet who is largely found in red-brick and established research institutions with brief glimpses of him on survey courses and elsewhere: *Social Chaucer* (Strohm, 1989), *Chaucer's Sexual Poetics* (Dinshaw, 1989), *Chaucer's Cultural Geography* (Lynch, 2002), *Chaucer's Queer Nation* (Burger, 2003). What man artow indeed.

Literary Politics

It is 1407. Lewis John the Welshman is hosting a dinner at his London home. The occasion is a gathering of prominent vintners. His close friend Thomas Chaucer may be there. Geoffrey Chaucer's old friend Henry Scogan certainly is. He is reading out his poem *Moral Balade*, dedicated to the Prince of Wales (later Henry V) and his brothers. In it he cites a number of lines from Chaucer's short work 'Gentilesse'. Here Chaucer insists that nobility is inherent, a virtue demonstrated in action and not inherited along with lands and title, a principle, he says, that applies even to those who wear 'mytre, crowne, or diadem'. This is the year in which Thomas Arundel begins to draft his repressive *Constitutions*, where he declares that a bishop's mitre and crozier symbolise his absolute power, the same year that Thomas Chaucer, Speaker, challenges him in open Parliament. Gathered at this dinner are those still loyal to a lost Ricardian regime, their hopes now centred on the Prince of Wales, Richard II's beloved surrogate son and the future King Henry V who, when he comes to power, will reward the Beauforts, those children of Gaunt and Katherine Swynford, Chaucer's nieces and nephews.

In the first decade after his death Chaucer's name acquired not just literary standing but political capital too. The same people repeatedly affirm his work: Hoccleve, writer and Lancastrian supporter; John Lydgate, close ally of Thomas Chaucer;

and Richard's former knights and other friends of Geoffrey – Henry Scogan, John Clanvowe, Peter Bukton, Lewis Clifford, Philip de la Vache. Often *their* work is attached to Chaucer's as part of his apocryphal canon, just as Chaucer dedicates or references them. *The Envoy to Bukton* is for Peter Bukton, a fellow witness in the Scrope-Grosvenor trial who also accompanied Chaucer on military campaigns with John of Gaunt. Henry Scogan is the dedicatee of another *Envoy* poem, while Chaucer's *Truth* is written for Philip de la Vache. That poem is a thinly veiled reference to the 1388 'deposition' of Richard by the Lords Appellant in which Chaucer advises him to look to his own self and beware the dangers of social climbing. Vache resigned as Keeper of the King's Parks in October 1386 and, like Chaucer, does not reappear in the records until Richard is properly restored to the throne.

In the royal courts that Chaucer inhabited, literature and politics worked hand in hand. In the preface to his *A Treatise on the Astrolabe*, Chaucer declares Richard II as the guardian of the English language in recognition of his support for the arts and championing of a vernacular already witnessed in European courts as a means of staking both literary and political territories. One positive aspect of the Hundred Years War was a rich interchange between French and English courtiers and writers. The French chronicler Jean Froissart came to the English court in 1362 as Queen Philippa of Hainault's secretary. The French King Jean II (Jean le Bon) was captured at Poitiers in 1356 and held hostage in Edward III's court. Jean brought with him poets like Guillaume de Machaut, while his son Jean Duc de Berry – who was exchanged for him at one time – was famed for his patronage of the arts. The well-known Savoyard knight Oton de Grandson also frequented English royal circles. He worked with Gaunt in the 1370s and again in the '90s. In between time he inhabited the French court where he was close to Chaucer's admirer Eustache Deschamps. Oton de Grandson led an international circle of literate diplomats originally founded by Philip de Mèzieres who had links to the Italian poets Petrarch and Boccaccio. This group shared books and other literary influences, some of which undoubtedly came Chaucer's way. His friend Lewis Clifford was a member of this circle and a frequent emissary between Deschamps and the English court.

The cosmopolitan courts of Richard and Edward clearly suited Chaucer. His early works in particular are heavily influenced by a French literary tradition. In a manuscript of French love lyrics (MS French 15, University of Pennsylvania, c. 1400) are fifteen works signed with the initial 'Ch' – probably 'Chaucer'. We know that he translated three of Oton de Grandson's poems as part of his own 'The Complaint of Venus'. It is also likely that he translated some part of the seminal French work *The Romance of the Rose* for *The Romaunt of the Rose*. Later work on *The Canterbury Tales* certainly shows the *Rose*'s influence. The Wife of Bath is Chaucer's version of La Vieille, the cynical old woman who tells how she tricked men in her youth, while the sardonic and scatological Faux-Semblant is the prototype for the outrageous Pardoner. More generally, the *Rose* sparked Chaucer's abiding interest in matters of destiny, free will and *gentillesse*. Chaucer's first major work, *The Book of the Duchess*, was written soon after the death of Blanche, John of Gaunt's first wife, in 1368, and is a poem of consolation that turns on the hunting of the heart/hart. Though it is in English, it remains greatly indebted to *The Romance of the Rose*, Froissart's *Paradis d'Amours* and, above all, the work of Machaut, especially his *Jugement dou Roy de Behaingne*.

Italian poetry also greatly influenced Chaucer's writing. He travelled to Italy twice on King's business, once in the early '70s and again in 1378. On that occasion he made a private trip to Florence and, we think, acquired copies of the works that inspired him so much: Boccaccio's *Teseida* and his *Il Filostrato* which is the main source for *Troilus and Criseyde*. Chaucer's next long poem was certainly not written before 1374, when he was still working at the customs. *The House of Fame* is incomplete in all of its surviving manuscripts – though, of course, none of these are authorial copies. Like *The Book of the Duchess*, it seems not to have been professionally copied, which means that Chaucer did not really begin to 'publish' and circulate his work until *Troilus and Criseyde*. *The House of Fame* is a consideration of the nature of poetry and reputation. Chaucer's narrator is carried off by an eagle that takes him up to a giant cage made of twigs and rumours where he meets the goddess who arbitrarily dispenses or withholds fame.

Chaucer composed *The House of Fame*, *The Parliament of Fowls*, 'The Knight's Tale' (for *The Canterbury Tales*) and *Troilus and Criseyde* in the same twelve-year period. *Troilus* retells the story of Troy through the secret love affair between Criseyde and Prince Troilus. Often described as the first modern novel, it was written somewhere between 1381–6 and is the pinnacle of Chaucer's career. During this time he also translated Boethius' *The Consolation of Philosophy*, as *Boece*. *The Legend of Good Women* came shortly after *Troilus*, in 1386, and is fictional penance for writing of Criseyde's abandonment of her lover. The last ten years of Chaucer's life were devoted to his ongoing project *The Canterbury Tales* with its range of voices and acute social observation, and to the majority of those short, 'political' poems mentioned throughout this biography.

In literary terms Chaucer's achievement is huge. His legacy was the classic English metre, the ten-syllable iambic pentameter he adapted from the French form – usually credited to Shakespeare. He introduced the rime-royal stanza and the *terza rima* into English poetry and sparked a tradition of vernacular writing. At the same time, his work remains inextricably linked to the political intrigues, faction-making and struggles for power of the Ricardian court and, later, the Lancastrian agenda of the future Henry V. Chaucer's death was merely the continuation, even the beginning, of a long and controversial life.

Conclusion

By 1437 Chaucer's son Thomas and Thomas' wife Maud were both dead. Chaucer's only grandchild Alice married twice, the second time to the powerful William de la Pole, Earl of Suffolk. He was disgraced and subsequently murdered in 1450. Alice tried, without success, to arrange a union between her eldest child John de la Pole (b. 1442) and Margaret Beaufort. She then switched allegiance to side with the Yorkists during the English civil War of the Roses. Chaucer's long-standing connection to the Lancastrians was over. His great-grandson John de la Pole eventually married one of the daughters of Richard, Duke of York in 1458 and was favoured by Henry VII until his death in 1494. After that, all of John's sons died or were beheaded. By 1539, shortly after Thynne's publication of Chaucer's *Workes* (1532), the male line of the de la Poles had petered out and Geoffrey Chaucer was dead and gone.

Despite the lack of hard facts and continuous documentary evidence, we know more about Geoffrey Chaucer than about any other medieval writer, more even than William Shakespeare. We know that he was one of the first authors to write in English at a time when England was still subject to a lasting legacy of Norman-French rule. We know that he was one of the first medieval writers to begin to sign his work, possibly one of the first whose name sold books. Chaucer's poetic achievements occurred at the intersection of print and oral cultures – when manuscripts might still be lost, damaged or edited – and at a time of profound change in the process of authoring, attribution, circulation, even commodification of literary works.

What we don't know is the extent to which his works, with their merest flickers of real-life disingenuous narrative and competing voices, illuminate the man. Both the peculiar context of his poetic achievement, and the gaps in our knowledge of his life, suggest that we can speculate and improvise about the man – and we do. Those early editors and compilers who collated Chaucer's manuscripts frequently co-opted him for agendas both literary and political, a process continued by later critics and biographers.

Many modern biographers admit the difficulties of uncovering the 'real' Chaucer. Yet even the most scholarly, aware and seemingly disinterested ones undermine that premise to assert that, in Derek Pearsall's words, 'the quality of his poetic presence... stimulates in us an unusually powerful desire to know what he was "really" like', and, moreover, to claim that he presents such a clear, consistent notion of identity 'as a person' that we feel 'he would have been worth knowing, and his views worth hearing'. Peter Ackroyd's imaginative suppositions and recreations strive to find a 'coherent picture' of the man buried beneath a mass of contradictions and through repeated reliance on a host of 'we can imagine' details. He reconstructs 'Chaucer's world' with its bustling London port unloading fish, salt, fuel, corn, the Friday Street fish market or scent of baking in Bread Street to give us a sensory overload reminiscent of another commodified, more modern Geoffrey Chaucer, accessed via the Canterbury Tales Experience in Canterbury, home of Chaucer's *Tales*. It is in real-life London, Ackroyd contends, that Chaucer found impetus for his work, 'intrigued by crowds and processions... in love with spectacle of every description and with the external life of humankind'. Ackroyd concludes that Chaucer was a sensitive bookworm who comes to us 'as if he fled from his own experience into the realms of art', a dreamy bystander not easily squared with the meticulous civil servant whose political acuity, or at least, exceptional prescience and good fortune, served him well in litigious and turbulent times.

If Ackroyd employs his own historical sensibilities and knowledge of late medieval life to create a Chaucer from a half-baked and insubstantial correlation of art and experience, Derek Pearsall looks to Chaucer's works, even as he admits that Chaucer-the-man cannot be accessed in this way. Pearsall's is a literary-criticism biography. Like this biography, his commends Chaucer for his adroit negotiation of politically charged medieval life, aided, in Pearsall's view, by 'never mentioning anything controversial in his poetry' and 'the instinct of the artist'. Where others might find a cynical man-of-the-age, Pearsall presents Chaucer the poet, an ironic satirist critical of his age's ideologies yet ultimately endorsing them.

Yet Pearsall, like others before him – and me after him – cannot finally resist the lure of constructing a Chaucer of his own out of nothing substantial. Ackroyd's modest, self-effacing and good-humoured man resembles Pearsall's genial, circumspect one who succeeds because he is 'clever, funny and inoffensive' and a 'decent sort of fellow', something every biographer eventually discovers, allegedly. If the man 'worth knowing' exists at all – and here I am guilty of the same uneasy imaginings as everyone else – then, for me, his successful courtliness and political savvy are somewhat repellent. I am suspicious of the careful observations, calculations and manipulations required by anyone who survives three kingships unscathed. So, too, I am ambivalent about any attempt to construct a definitive Chaucer biography (an ultimately impossible task), even as I remain interested in its mystery and compelled by the quality and legacy of his writing.

I began research for this book certain that I would find no trace of the man between the lines of his poetry. My interest in him has always been academic, refracted through a postmodern perspective and the contemporary critical lens of gender and queer theory. I now find myself certain that despite the absence of obvious keynote references in his work – why would he be so stupid? – here is a writer crucially engaged with the dissents and debates of his time, no more a genial liberal humanist than he is the affable, laugh-a-minute, sex-mad author of the *fabliaux*. Instead, he is a writer acutely conscious of how to position himself, both in literary and in social terms. I now think that the best way to read this clever and slippery man is with an awareness of how his work is closely enmeshed in late medieval culture.

In many respects, Geoffrey Chaucer remains an enigma. As Steve Ellis has noted, his presence is significant yet diffuse, scattered throughout a contemporary popular culture that uses him to mediate 'merry England', and conflicts with a formidable yet shrinking presence in the academy. What remains is the 'elvish' outsider slowly receding from view, 'pushed to the margins' of his 'own fictionalized life story', forever beckoning, and yet always guaranteed to disappear from view. I still think he was too sharp to be anything other than grudgingly admirable: a perspicacious politician, upwardly mobile, learned and well connected, a courtier with an eye for the main chance and an unerring instinct for self-preservation. Beneath the mask of the dream-vision narrators' wide-eyed innocence and 'don't blame me' is perhaps a truth closer than we imagine: the detached observer, his finger on the pulse of medieval culture, always on the sidelines, careful never to get caught. He knew kings' secrets. He escaped rebellions unscathed, almost to the last. I do not believe he was murdered but I do think he was taken unawares knowing that the tide was turning and that his manuscripts might be next on the list. He was taking steps – interrupted – to secure his welfare, just as he always did. I think he would be more than satisfied with his afterlives.

Chronological List of Works

Late 1360s   Possibly *The Romaunt of the Rose*, translation
of part of the French *Roman de la Rose*
Some poems in French?
The ABC, a Marian devotion poem (though this
may be a '90s poem)

1368–9   *The Book of the Duchess*

1378   Finished *The House of Fame*

c. 1380–6   *The Parliament of Fowls*
Palamon and Arcite ('The Knight's Tale')
Troilus and Criseyde
Boece
Short poems: 'Adam Scriveyn', 'The Complaint
of Mars', 'The Complaint of Venus', 'Truth',
'Gentilesse', 'Lak of Stedfastnesse'

c. 1386–7   *The Legend of Good Women* (Prologue revised 1394–5)
Begins *The Canterbury Tales*

1391   *A Treatise on the Astrolabe*

1396–1400   Short poems: 'Envoy to Bukton', 'Envoy to
Scogan', 'The Complaint of Chaucer to His Purse'
The Canterbury Tales is still ongoing

Bibliography

Biographical detail has been taken, in the main, from the *Chaucer Life-Records* (1966)

Peter Ackroyd, *Chaucer: Brief Lives* (London, 2005)

D.S. Brewer (ed.), *Chaucer, The Critical Heritage*, 2 vols. (London, 1978)

G.K. Chesterton, *Chaucer* (London, 1932)

Nevill Coghill, *Geoffrey Chaucer* (London, 1956)

Martin M. Crow and Clair C. Olson, *Chaucer Life-Records* (Oxford, 1966)

Steve Ellis, *Chaucer At Large: The Poet in the Modern Imagination* (Minneapolis and London, 2000)

Kathleen Forni, *The Chaucerian Apocrypha: A Counterfeit Canon* (Gainesville, 2001)

F.J. Furnivall, 'Trial Forewords to My "Parallel-Text" Edition of Chaucer's Minor Poems', *Chaucer Society*, second series 6, 1871

'Recent Work at Chaucer', *Macmillan's Magazine* 27 (1872–3), pp. 383–88

Terry Jones et al., *Who Murdered Chaucer? A Medieval Mystery* (London, 2003)

Derek Pearsall, *The Life of Geoffrey Chaucer: A Critical Biography* (Oxford, 1992)

Walter Skeat, *The Chaucer Canon: with a discussion of the works associated with the name of Geoffrey Chaucer* (Oxford, 1900)

Biographical note

Gail Ashton is a writer, editor and former university lecturer in medieval and contemporary literature. Recent publications include *Chaucer: A Reader's Guide* (Continuum, 2007) and *Medieval Romance in Context* (Continuum, 2010). Her second poetry collection is forthcoming from Cinnamon Press, as is a co-edited volume on medieval afterlives in popular culture (Palgrave) for which she is writing on the BBC series *Torchwood*. She is also series co-editor for Continuum's *Texts and Contexts*.

SELECTED TITLES FROM HESPERUS PRESS

Brief Lives

Author	Title
Anthony Briggs	*Brief Lives: Leo Tolstoy*
Andrew Brown	*Brief Lives: Gustave Flaubert*
Andrew Brown	*Brief Lives: Stendhal*
Richard Canning	*Brief Lives: E.M. Forster*
Richard Canning	*Brief Lives: Oscar Wilde*
David Carter	*Brief Lives: Honoré de Balzac*
Robert Chandler	*Brief Lives: Alexander Pushkin*
Melissa Valiska Gregory and Melisa Klimaszewski	*Brief Lives: Charles Dickens*
Gavin Griffiths	*Brief Lives: Joseph Conrad*
Patrick Miles	*Brief Lives: Anton Chekhov*
Andrew Piper	*Brief Lives: Johann Wolfgang von Goethe*
Alan Shelston	*Brief Lives: Elizabeth Gaskell*
Fiona Stafford	*Brief Lives: Jane Austen*

Classics and Modern Voices

Author	Title	Foreword writer
Honoré de Balzac	*Colonel Chabert*	A.N. Wilson
Honoré de Balzac	*Sarrasine*	Kate Pullinger
Honoré de Balzac	*The Vendetta*	
Marquis de Sade	*Virtue*	
Stendhal	*Memoirs of an Egotist*	Doris Lessing
Stendhal	*On love*	A.C. Grayling